DOUBLE
LIVES

For permission requests, please contact the publisher at:

Mango Publishing Group
2850 Douglas Road, 3rd Floor
Coral Gables, FL 33134 U.S.A.
info@mango.bz

For special orders, quantity sales, course adoptions and corporate sales, please email the publisher at sales@mango.bz. For trade and wholesale sales, please contact Ingram Publisher Services at: customer.service@ingramcontent.com or +1.800.509.4887.

Double Lives: True Tales of the Criminals Next Door

Library of Congress Cataloging
ISBN: (p) 978-1-63353-780-4, (e) 978-1-63353-781-1
Library of Congress Control Number: 2018947701
BISAC—TRU000000—TRUE CRIME / General

Printed in the United States of America.

DOUBLE LIVES

True Tales of the Criminals Next Door

ERIC BRACH

Mango Publishing
CORAL GABLES, FL

CONTENTS

FOREWORD   6

INTRODUCTION   8

CHAPTER 1   15
Eagle Rock, CA—John Leonard Orr

CHAPTER 2   26
Investigations

CHAPTER 3   31
Broomall, PA—Carl Gugasian

CHAPTER 4   40
Mansfield, TX—David Graham and Diane Zamora

CHAPTER 5   54
Bath Township, MI—Andrew Kehoe

CHAPTER 6   66
Mountain City, TN—Jenelle Potter

CHAPTER 7   74
Evan

CHAPTER 8   83
New York City—Louis Eppolito

CHAPTER 9   95
Manchester, NJ—Joseph S. Portash

CHAPTER 10 106
Kerrville, TX—Genene Jones

CHAPTER 11 124
Chillicothe, MO—Ray & Faye Copeland

CHAPTER 12 138
Evan (Continued)

CHAPTER 13 147
Ft. Myers, FL—Kevin Foster

CHAPTER 14 160
Sacramento, CA—Theresa Knorr

CHAPTER 15 175
Raleigh, NC—Carlette Parker

CHAPTER 16 187
Park City, KS—Dennis Rader

CHAPTER 17 200
Yorkville, IL—Dennis Hastert

CONCLUSION 211

ACKNOWLEDGMENTS 215

BIBLIOGRAPHY 216

ABOUT THE AUTHOR 232

FOREWORD

—

When a violent criminal strikes, it is human nature to seek solace in a reason…a justification…an explanation—something logical and tangible that we can grasp onto to convince ourselves that there is something that separates the perpetrators and victims in the gruesome news reports from the safety and tranquility of our daily lives, something to explain how and why someone would do something so horrific, so unimaginable. That's what allows us to put our children to sleep at night, convincing ourselves that such violent acts could never happen to our loved ones.

Having spent over a decade as a Deputy District Attorney prosecuting some of the most violent and senseless crimes in the largest prosecutorial agency in the nation, I have found myself asking the same questions hundreds, if not thousands, of times. What is it that separates me from those criminals who sit just feet away from me at the other side of counsel table? What turn did they take in their lives that I did not? How did they end up in the same room as me but on a very different side of that table? Surely there is something obvious—some mark, some sign, some characteristic—that could be discerned by the most casual observer to explain this divergence? Unfortunately, these are questions that remain unanswered.

Double Lives brilliantly illustrates this chilling truth. There often are no signs, n o obvious indicators that separate the pleasant neighbor from the sadistic murderer. As the book documents so well, the scary reality is that a criminal rarely fits the profile we have in our mind's eye, and our own sense of safety and security is simply illusory.

As a prosecuting attorney confronted with this reality on a daily basis, I am often at a loss to explain such depraved acts to a jury hell-bent on finding a motive before they can understand and punish such acts of human brutality. Alas, I too often turn to the only explanation I have, which is that there is none. Sometimes people who can easily blend into your church group, softball team, or PTA meeting commit acts of stomach-wrenching depravity simply for the thrill of the crime.

It is this lack of explanation that makes the stories in *Double Lives* so chilling. In the end, we are left with the unsettling vulnerability of what we do not want to admit: that it could have been us.

Double Lives is a great insight into the minds of the wolves in sheep's clothing. While we aren't left with an answer as to why these things happen—why seemingly everyday people are compelled to commit unspeakable acts of evil—we are given an inimitable inside look into the minds of the criminals and the people left in their wake.

Rachel Bowers, LA County Deputy District Attorney

May 2018

INTRODUCTION

—

Three of my friends from high school are dead. Four more are felons.

They are why this book exists. Not the dead ones—the criminals.

I imagine that in many parts of the country—including Los Angeles, where I now live and teach—it's not that crazy for any given high school to produce a few kids each year who end up in jail, and a few more who are stuck beneath the dirt before their time. Where I grew up, though, it felt impossible.

I'm from central Long Island. Nassau County. The median household income there is one of the highest in the country, and the little village where I grew up is idyllic. Only half an hour from New York City, there are no stoplights, and the only business is a plant nursery.

It has its own police force, too. They're not that busy.

The local public high school I went to had more in common with *90210* than with the real world. There were Japanese classes, and seventeen-year-old kids drove luxury SUVs off campus to get pizza from Vincent's at lunch. When I was a senior, we got written up in *Newsweek* as being the best high school in the country.

Crime? Death? Our school wasn't the sort of place where those things happened. The nearest thing we had to tragedy was when one kid had cancer. He beat it, of course, coming back to class in a wheelchair for months before making a full recovery and becoming the starting center on the basketball team and leading it all the way to the state championships. A few years later, another kid developed a tumor behind his eyeball—he beat his disease, too, and grew up to become one of the top wrestlers in the country.

It was like living in an after-school special. Even our hard times turned out for the best.

As for the kids who actually died, they were all good enough to wait to do so until after graduation, in their early twenties. Their deaths were sad, but also not uncommon. One had a congenital health defect that caught up to him. A second died in a car wreck, and not long after that one passed, his identical twin brother killed himself, unable to stand the grief.

In all, unfortunate—tragic—but totally understandable. Explainable. Which is probably why the crimes shook me so much more than the deaths. They seemed so unimaginable, so surreal.

One guy, who'd been in my class's student government, was arrested for statutory rape—he used MySpace to have sex with an underage girl. He was twenty-five. She was fifteen.

Another guy, who'd been on my Little League team when we were kids, carjacked a heroin dealer at gunpoint from the parking lot of our local diner. The dealer called the cops because he didn't realize it was a setup; he thought the other people in his car were getting kidnapped along with his ride, his cash, and his stash. Every one of them ended up in jail.

A third guy, with whom I'd played in a Battle of the Bands, got spotted breaking into some acquaintances' apartment. (One of the songs we'd played was a cover of "The Freshmen" by The

Verve Pipe, which will explain an awful lot to other children of the '90s about the kind of teenagers we'd been.) He fled, but when the burglary victims asked him to come back to talk it over, he returned to the scene of the crime—right into the waiting arms of the police.

The fourth was the kid brother of my closest friend in eighth grade. When we were little, he'd hang out with us as we played basketball and street hockey. When he grew up, he took part in a scam cell phone racket, peppering Long Island with knockoff Apple and Motorola handsets smuggled in from abroad and assembled from counterfeit parts. The Immigration and Customs Enforcement bust eventually turned up thousands of bogus smartphones and hundreds of thousands of dollars in stacked and bundled cash.

Learning about these crimes shocked me. Part of the it was that these people I thought I'd known had done these things at all. These were all low and hurtful acts, the kind of misdeeds I might have expected out of *someone else*—some misfit from far, far away—but never from people I knew, never from people I grew up with. How was it that these four had developed from friends and classmates into people who went on to commit such heinous crimes right in my—right in *our*—backyard?

But even after the shock wore off, something about these crimes still bothered me. It took me a while to figure it out, but I realized that what stuck with me was how nobody seemed to have known what was happening—nobody had so much as guessed at the road these people were on until they'd reached the end of it. Hell, I only even found about what these guys had done after reading about their crimes on the *internet*. When classmates died, I heard about it through word-of-mouth; the ones who went to jail, though, I only learned about once they were caught and outsiders exposed them. Until then, nobody knew—or even suspected—what they'd been up to. They seemed for all the world to be just like everybody else. Somehow, they'd been developing into the criminals they became right under the noses of their friends and family, and nobody knew until it was too late.

The more I thought about it, the more I began to wonder: how many others are out there who are just the same? How many people live among us, right under our noses, and turn out bad—or do bad—without our knowledge? How many people are there that we work with, that we see every day, who are keeping secret from us a horrible double life?

•

I started *Double Lives* with the intent of simply writing about these kinds of people—criminals who lived, worked, and in some cases had a family in the very towns where they grew up. I created a list of some of the worst Americans I could find, people who, every day, hid their true selves from those around them as they perpetrated some of the worst crimes imaginable. As I grew to learn more about what they'd done, I found myself heartbroken, equal parts revolted and horrified at the depths a human being can sink to. (And if I've done my job correctly, so will you.) But as I wrote, two things happened:

One, I kept finding myself thinking about the people I'd known from my own hometown—for a number of reasons.

And two, I realized that something that linked all these people—both the true sociopaths and the ones I'd known as everyday teens who evolved into something far different. It was that people knew them but just didn't see.

In the foreword to his short story collection *Night Shift*, Stephen King wrote:

> *At night, when I go to bed, I still am at pains to be sure that my legs are under the blanket after the lights go out.*
> *I'm not a child any more, but I don't like to sleep with one leg sticking out. Because if a cool hand ever reached out from under the bed and grasped my ankle, I might scream. Yes, I might scream to wake the dead. That sort of thing doesn't happen, of course, and we all know that.... The thing under my bed waiting to grab my ankle isn't real.*
> *I know that, and I also know that if I'm careful to keep my foot under the covers, it will never be able to grab my ankle.*

Most people (excepting those who work in the justice system) will never knowingly come face-to-face with a criminal. To most people, in fact, the subjects profiled in this book might seem close cousins to Stephen King's monsters: horrible beasts, figments from our nightmares divorced from our lives. But in truth, our lives—the very existences we've built around us—*are* our blankets. We drape them over ourselves, even all the way above our heads, so we don't have worry about the monsters grabbing for our ankles—but that doesn't mean they're not out there. Indeed, until they were caught, most of the people in this book wore masks that showed a rosy face—but underneath, they were monsters. Real monsters.

As real as a heart defect. Or a car crash. Or a suicide.

The more I wrote, the more I found that these two disparate threads became woven together in my mind. I started out intending only to profile some of the most unusual double life-leading criminals of twentieth-century America, but as I did, I began to think deeply about certain people from my picture-perfect high school who would later go down the wrong road. Eventually, little parts of my own experience began to sneak in.

I should point out that I make no claims to know why some people act the way they do. I believe I am spectacularly underqualified to do so, and there are countless books about that already, besides. No, these one-time peers inspired me to look for other people following the same path they tread: living double lives, flirting with crime and addiction, fooling those nearest to them into thinking they lived one way while secretly lurking on a parallel plane.

I mentioned that I teach. All of my students have self-selected into a pre-professional program that aims to train them to better their communities, and many end up becoming law enforcement officers. Over the years, I've found that they're more likely to complete their assignments when they're interested in what they're reading, so I'll admit: I'd love it if any of them bother to read this book. Certainly, there are enough case studies here to hold the attention of those who are simply interested in reading true crime. (Wherever possible, I've relied on primary sources— including conversations and interviews I've had with those close to the cases—to drive the narratives of these histories, utilizing information from secondary sources as needed to fill in the blanks.

For academic readers like them, a complete bibliography has been made available at the end of the text.)

But this book isn't really not for those kids—or at least, not for them alone. Most of this book pulls back the curtain on some of America's worst sociopaths, but a small part of it details a very personal process in trying to understand how a regular person can become the cause of their own ruin—and just like a dyed-in-the-wool criminal, do it right under everyone's nose. To my surprise, that tiny part required just as much work as the rest, because it forced me to ruminate on a very real, very difficult trend that's growing more prevalent in our nation by the day—not just *out there*, not just far away, but everywhere. Even my TV-perfect hometown.

In that regard, this book is for anyone who's willing to brave lifting the blanket, leaning over the edge, and checking under the bed to learn about the darkness possible in the world. Because like it or not, the monsters are there.

And they are not alone.

CHAPTER 1

—

Eagle Rock, CA—John Leonard Orr

You might say it started in October, 1984, at a home-and-crafts store in South Pasadena called Ole's, pronounced more like the name of a Minnesota fisherman than a cry in a bullring. That's certainly where the fire started, anyhow, and when. But really, it began much, much earlier.

Generally, arsonists are white and male, and they tend to have family problems, particularly issues with women. While they often set their fires in post-pubescence in an attempt to retaliate against a real or imagined injustice, such as a professional or personal slight, the arsonists themselves generally catch the fire bug during their youth. More often than not, they're exposed to a formative event or events that leave them fascinated by flames.

John Leonard Orr was a captain in the Glendale Fire Department, a district serving the area north of Los Angeles. Prior to that, he'd been an arson investigator, also in Glendale, a suburb abutting his hometown of Eagle Rock, where he'd grown up and seen a couch catch on fire in his friend's living room, nearly burning the house down with all inside.

On the other side of Eagle Rock is South Pasadena, where on one night in October, 1984, Ole's was set ablaze.

Ole's was a local chain that sold all kinds of DIY and decorative goods: yarn for knitting, glue for assembling model kits, and polyurethane foam for shaping dollhouse bedding and supporting flower displays. It was in this last section—the polyurethane foam, made from oil and gas byproducts and eminently flammable—that the first fire began.

"I was walking toward the front of the store and I noticed…a grayish-white pillar of smoke," said Jim Obdam, a teenager who'd been working the cash register there. "I looked down one of the side aisles…there was just a wall of flames. I felt trapped."

Within moments, the whole building caught fire. South Pasadena Engine Company 81, led by Fire Captain William Eisele, was called to fight the blaze. His team was understaffed, because there appeared to have been another fire that had sparked off moments earlier at a Von's grocery store, and still another an hour before that at an Albertson's a few miles north. They were almost incapable of stanching the blaze, they were so shorthanded. Imagine his surprise, then, when Eisele was approached by a man dressed in plainclothes but who claimed to be a firefighter. He claimed to be "just passing by," but he volunteered to take photos for department records and investigative purposes, an offer that Eisele accepted.

That man was John Leonard Orr.

•

John Orr was born in 1949, raised in the Southern California canyons where the unceasing dry heat and the Santa Ana winds can put a lot of pressure on both fragile ecosystems and tenuous marriages. By the time John was in high school, his mother had abandoned the family without a word, and John, the youngest of three boys, was left looking for a way out. He joined the Air Force, hoping to escape, but it was not to be. John spent the Vietnam War in a special division tasked with stanching fires caused by plane crashes, and by the time his midtwenties rolled around, he found himself twice divorced, barely employed, and still stuck in the Los Angeles foothills.

Despite Orr's military and firefighting background, he'd been rejected by the LAPD, the LA County Sheriff's Department, and both the LA city and county fire bureaus. With LA fire, he failed the physical; he'd neglected to study or train, grossly overconfident that his years in military service would carry him through. With the LAPD, he failed the psych exam. They said he was "unsuitable." They said he had an "unstable personality."

They didn't know the half of it.

After getting turned down for all the LA public service jobs to which he'd applied, Orr accepted a lowly position as a mall security guard at a Sears, a career path that at least offered him the chance to collar lawbreakers and access to a concealed weapons permit. In short order, he developed a taste for both. He eventually did secure a municipal job, finding a home in the comparatively low-paying and none-too-prestigious Glendale Fire Department. All the same, he kept pursuing criminals, hoping to make a name for himself.

"He hung out in cop bars and wore an ankle holster with a semiautomatic gun attached," read an article in the Glendale Post–Dispatch, "despite a fire department rule banning weapons from department vehicles. He had a badge he could change from fire to police, passing himself off as a cop, and [he] busted everyone."

By the night of the fire at Ole's, Orr had put in ten years at the Glendale Fire Department but had few friends there. He'd built a reputation as a maverick, a wanna-be cop. And when the Ole's fire was ruled accidental by the fire investigators, he bucked, loudly disputing the official findings, seemingly desperate to find a bad guy and catch him. Obdam, the teen working the register, had escaped, but others weren't so lucky. Four people died in the structure fire that night, including a two-year-old shopping with his grandmother, and the very next day, Orr sought out Karen Berry, a family member of one of the fire's victims, and told her that he believed the fire was an act of arson, set in the section of the store that sold polyurethane foam.

How he was able to come to such a conclusion, he didn't say. But when another Ole's store caught on fire two months later—a fire that was indisputably determined to have started in the foam and padding housewares section—he successfully snuffed out any doubt.

As more and more fires touched off in these LA suburbs throughout the mid-1980s, Orr came to be taken as a fire genius. He began to be seen as someone who could pull clues from wreckage like a treasure hunter, with powers of deductive reasoning that far surpassed his peers, and he did his best to stoke these conclusions. He appeared ever more frequently on television, harnessing the power of local news broadcasts' hunger for scoops to position himself as a knowledgeable keeper of the shield, and he began to be asked to lead seminars for other firefighters, teaching them how arson spreads and how to combat it.

By the late '80s, Orr had been promoted to fire captain, and his meteoric rise dovetailed with the increasing frequency of suspicious conflagrations in stores throughout the suburbs north of LA. These outbursts continued intermittently and without a clear pattern until 1987, when a string of store fires broke out over the course of three days along State Route 99.

A Bakersfield fire investigator named Marvin Casey was charged with looking into these Route 99 crimes, and he found an important piece of evidence in the rubble: three charred matchsticks tied to a burnt cigarette with a rubber band, concealed in a singed piece of yellow legal paper. It was a delayed incendiary device, and a simple one: the arsonist could wrap it all up, light the cigarette, throw it somewhere, and leave. It would take time for the smoldering cigarette to burn down to the match heads: time for the arsonist to escape. When the match heads did catch, they'd flare, igniting the anything combustible nearby—say, perhaps, hydrocarbon-based polyurethane foam, the kind sold in craft stores and highly flammable. The paper tube would provide extra fuel for the flame once it lit as well as shield the device from prying eyes.

Remnants of similar, ingenious devices were found at other sites of suspicious fires along the highway, including in a pillow bin at a fabric shop and in a display of sleeping bags in a surplus store. Eventually, investigators were able to pull a fingerprint—one— off a piece of note paper found intact on one of these firestarters amongst the charred remains of a torched building. Though they couldn't find a match to a culprit in their criminal database, Marvin Casey had a hunch, and to understand it, you need to understand the California highways.

California's Route 99 originates a few miles east of the capitol building in Sacramento. It shoots southbound through Fresno,

Tulare, and Bakersfield before merging with I-5 somewhere in the state's largely uninhabited Antelope Valley; after that, the road continues onward to Los Angeles. The first of these Route 99 fires broke out in Bakersfield, near the southern terminus of the highway. It was followed soon thereafter by a spate of fires in Fresno, and after two days, similar fires in stores in Tulare and in Bakersfield once again. The arsonist, it seemed, had traveled up Route 99 from LA, started a few fires in broad daylight along the way, then stopped in Fresno for a few days to ply his trade before returning back south. And during those two days, one particularly conspicuous gathering was taking place in Fresno: an annual convention of arson investigators.

Marvin Casey had a theory, a theory no firefighter wanted to hear: that this firebug, one of the most prolific and daring arsonists in America to date, was one of their own.

In 1989, a new string of fires broke out along a stretch of Highway 101, a road that runs from downtown LA all the way to Seattle; these coincided with another conference of arson investigators, this one held in Monterey Bay. Still, flames continued to ravage Southern California for two more years until, in 1991, investigators reached out to the LA Sheriff's Department to run the crime scene fingerprint against not just known criminals, but every fingerprint they held in their entire database—which included everyone who'd ever applied to work there.

Lo and behold, they got a match. This arsonist who liked to strike mid-day, during business hours, using matches tied to a cigarette with rubber bands and a paper roll, had the very same left ring finger print as fire captain John Leonard Orr.

•

According to most literature about the pathopsychological roots to arson, there are six primary reasons people set fires: profit, extremism, concealment of other crimes, vandalism, revenge, and excitement. All of these motivations are tied, in one way or another, to exercising or proving power, the last three in particular. What better way to show the world how tough you are than to unleash the unfettered strength of the elements? How better to prove someone wrong who misjudged your worth than by exhibiting your might in flame? And how better to bathe in love for one's own potency than to watch a blaze lick at a structure—natural or man-made—knowing that you are the source of all that follows?

Orr had seen fires when he was a kid—there'd been the incident with his neighbor's couch, as well as the time a trash can fire spread to an adjacent telephone pole and ran up the wires. In both cases, he'd watched firemen extinguish the flames and be lauded as heroes. He may have been spurned by multiple agencies *and* his own mother, but now, he was respected as an expert in his field.

After all, it had been he who first insisted that the murderous Ole's fire had not been an accident at all—hadn't it?

•

Prosecutors were prepared to charge John Orr with setting the spate of fires, but they had one problem: the charges might not stick. They could conclusively link him and his fingerprints to one blaze set years prior, but that was where their evidence ended—and what if Orr could come up with a feasible defense? They needed, they decided, to catch Orr in the act, so they could establish a pattern of activity and link Orr to all the crimes.

With the help of the FBI, investigators placed a tracking device on Orr's car, and almost immediately, they hit the jackpot. On the Friday before Thanksgiving, 1991, Orr parked his car on a street along the Warner Brothers studio backlot. Soon thereafter, a fire started and engulfed an unused film set. Orr sped back home, and when a call went out over the dispatch reporting the fire, Orr turned around and headed back for the fire.

That's when something unexpected happened. On air, the dispatcher accidentally provided the wrong address for the fire... yet Orr arrived at the right place anyway.

With this misstep, Orr had betrayed himself, and investigators immediately executed a warrant to search Orr's property. In his car, they found cigarettes, matches, rubber bands, and paper—the very recipe for the delayed incendiary devices that their serial arsonist so liked. In his home, they found still more incriminating evidence. First, there was a VHS tape holding video footage of a house on a hillside engulfed in flames. This was a house ignited by the serial arsonist, and the footage had been, officially, shot for investigation purposes. However, rewinding the tape, investigators found home video footage of the house just starting to smolder, taken before anyone in the fire department had ever been reported as having arrived on the scene. Rewinding even further, they saw the same house, good as new, in video shot and dated over a year earlier.

It was the record of a hunt: the prey, the trap, and the inferno. But that wasn't all. Officers searching his house also found a manuscript written by Orr detailing the adventures of a fire investigator who turned arsonist and lit fires on his own.

Orr claimed the book was a novel, a work of fiction. However, the details of the fires written in the book perfectly matched the descriptions of the arsons that had occurred throughout Southern California throughout the past decade, the ones the serial arsonist was believed to have set. There was a fire at "Cal's," a hardware store just like the one at Ole's that had killed four people, and the protagonist, a man named Aaron Stiles, even used time-delay incendiary devices made of matches and cigarettes to start fires while on his way to and from arson conferences.

The protagonist's name—Aaron Stiles—was an anagram for the phrase, "I set LA arson."

•

In the ten years before John Leonard Orr was arrested, there were an average of sixty-seven fires per year in the hills above Glendale, Burbank, Eagle Rock, and Pasadena, the area where Orr grew up and worked. In the years after Orr's arrest, that annual average dropped from sixty-seven fires per year to just one.

John Orr, it turned out, was responsible for more than 95 percent of the fires in the town where he'd made his career and his name as a firefighter.

In 1991, Orr was tried and quickly convicted of a number of counts of arson related to his spree at the Fresno investigators' convention. He later pled guilty to others. In a separate proceeding, Orr was tried and convicted on four counts of first-degree murder for the deaths of the four people killed in the '84 fire at Ole's. He was spared the death penalty, but he is currently serving life without the possibility of parole in the California State Penitentiary System.

Orr would later appeal his murder convictions, asserting that items such as the matches, cigarettes, rubber bands, and lighters found in his car—along with the book that he wrote—should not have been admissible in court, because they might have prejudiced the jury against him. The appeals court, however, noted that some things do indeed affect a jury's perception of the accused, and often, those things are called evidence. It is true that hoarding all of the items used to start fires—to say nothing about writing a book about a firefighter arsonist with a thinly-veiled version of yourself as the main character—may lead a jury to believe that you are guilty of arson. But it's not necessarily true that the jury shouldn't be able to see all that evidence, just because you were titillated enough, haughty enough, or just plain dumb enough to keep it at hand.

Noted true-crime writer Joseph Wambaugh wrote a book about John Orr, which he called *Fire Lover*. The title comes from the opening lines of Orr's own book, in which he writes about the power and thrill of starting a flame, "The fire becomes a mistress. A lover."

"He photographed the fires so that he could relive the event," said Wambaugh, "for the same reason that serial killers photograph their victims: so they can look at them later and relive the events."

John Leonard Orr spent the better part of a decade setting thousands of fires in the hills and buildings all around his Southern California hometown—killing four and causing billions of dollars' worth of damage—so he could sit back and watch. And sometimes tape. All for the thrill.

CHAPTER 2

Investigations

When I wrote in the introduction that three people from high school were dead, it was true. It isn't anymore. Now, five are gone.

Two more kids from my high school class have died in the short time from when I wrote the first sentence of this book to when I wrote this one. It was drug overdoses for both of them.

The first was a guy named Nick (a pseudonym). He had just turned thirty-five when he went. I found out he died when people from school started emailing each other—word-of-mouth—but at first, nobody knew how or why he'd gone.

Given that he was so young and that his death came as a shock even to people close to him, my first thought upon finding out was that it had either been drugs or he'd killed himself.

It felt terrible to think that, but all the signs seemed to point that way. For starters, he couldn't have been sick. Some friend of his from a Friday night bowling league sent an email to my high school alumni listserv, asking if anyone had info on how he'd passed. Apparently, he bowled one week and just didn't show up the next. The guy didn't even know Nick died and was trying to find out what happened.

That's why I figured he couldn't have been sick. People don't go out bowling one week and succumb to terminal illness the next. People on their deathbeds don't sign up for recreational sports leagues.

So it had to be sudden. A car crash might have made sense. But if it had been a car crash, it seemed like that would have been in an obituary or a news story somewhere, and I couldn't find anything like that—no information at all except that he was dead.

On his memorial webpage, hosted by the mortuary where he had his final services, people lit e-candles and wrote little goodbye notes, posting messages like "We lost a legend way too soon," and, "I wish you were here to see how much your coworkers honor you." But there was no extra information about what had happened. Just the pale fact of his death.

•

Later, I heard from Nick's family and those coworkers. It was, indeed, a drug overdose.

•

Nick worked at a supplement company—the kind that isn't regulated by the FDA. They advertise on TV and the radio, promising free, limited trial supplies of some miracle substance or another. It doesn't take long to find that there are quite a few complaints lodged against the company with the Better Business Bureau and on online message boards from customers who sent away for free stuff, then got shoved onto auto-delivery lists with fresh bottles of pills delivered monthly until they canceled, by which time they'd generally accidentally purchased a couple hundred or even thousand dollars' worth of unwanted supplements.

So all right, Nick's job was none too prestigious—but it was a job all the same. He had coworkers, and they liked him. He had teammates, and he had friends. He'd even just had a birthday. And in the weeks before he died, he walked past these people every day, always keeping a secret hiding just below the surface—both a secret of his past and a secret of his future, of the horrible thing he was doing until it claimed him for good.

I started to wonder: what must that have been like? That pressure, trying to keep people in the dark every day, right up until his last?

•

This is another thing I found out since I started working on this book: John Orr lives within driving distance from my house.

I wrote "lives," but maybe that's the wrong word. "Lives" implies some element of choice, like John Orr went apartment hunting and picked a place somewhere near me. I should phrase it another way.

John Orr is incarcerated within driving distance from my house.

That said, most of the people connected with Orr's case in fact do still live no more than a day's drive from me. The only exception is Marvin Casey, who moved to Texas to be closer to his grandkids.

I find this out from his Facebook page.

Even though Orr committed his crimes thirty-plus years ago, well before the widespread adoption of the internet, I had no trouble tracking down most of the people I hoped to talk to, even in this age where most of our work is completed entirely online. The ones who worked alongside him, the ones who investigated him, the ones who brought him down—they're all out there, and they were all happy to discuss the case with me. To my surprise, this would far more often than not hold true with everyone I profiled: it seems there are always people—neighbors, relatives, descendants—willing to share their recollections and reflections, if only someone will ask.

Pat Hanly, the DA who first got a conviction on John Orr, was the first person to speak with me about any of the criminals in this book. He'd left the civil service and had become a private defense lawyer in Sacramento. As I understand it, defense lawyers always teach their clients to never offer up anything unless necessary—but when the subject of John Orr came up, we were off to the races. Hanly shared with me not only his impressions of Orr, but also information about the case I otherwise never could have known. He told me about Orr's flimsy first attempts at a defense, which hinged on a billing statement for a pay-per-view movie at his Fresno hotel, as well as his own recollections of sitting around his office with ATF agents, redacting material from Orr's steamy novel for trial.

Chris Gray, now a Pasadena fire captain and formerly the Assistant Chief in Glendale during Orr's time there, described for me how he came to be in the unusual position of being a witness both for the prosecution and the defense during the trials. "I was of the mind that I wanted to see justice served," Gray told me. "Of course you have a civic duty, and I was subpoenaed, so I was going to testify one way or the other...but in the sentencing phase, I volunteered to testify for both the prosecution and the defense." I asked him why, and he said, "Well, they were going for the death penalty. It's one thing to talk about capital punishment, but it's another thing to participate in it."

Glen Lucero, an LAFD arson investigator who, like John, had come up through the Air Force before entering the civil fire service and knew Orr personally, shared with me what it was like to be involved in the investigations as they were underway—what it was like to work alongside John Orr in those last days having to pretend that he didn't already know who Orr really was, just as Orr spent all those years pretending he was something else.

Mike Matassa, who headed up the ATF investigation into Orr, shared in great detail how he and Glen Lucero interviewed witnesses to get the information that proved Orr's guilt. At the end, he said something that stuck with me. "Anyone is capable of anything," he said. "Anyone can be fooled. And sociopaths are good at fooling people."

It was a very raw and real take, one that I wrote down and which came back to me later when I found myself out shopping for new bed pillows. I was stuffing them against my face to test if they were comfy enough, and when I looked around I realized that I was in the foam section of a large department store, all alone in an aisle that was blocked off from sight of the rest of the building.

Basically, John Orr's hunting ground.

I put down the pillows. I quickly left, buying nothing. Walking out of the store's sliding glass doors, it was the second time I found myself faced with the thought that, as much as this book is about criminals, there might end up being a little bit of my own experience in it as well.

CHAPTER 3

—

Broomall, PA—Carl Gugasian

Carl Gugasian's story reads like an episode of *Scooby-Doo*: a reign of terror and a string of crimes, all masterminded by a man in a mask.

And he would have gotten away with it, too, if it weren't for those meddling kids.

Picture Southeastern Pennsylvania: it sits awash in sprawling leas and historic woodlands. The exurbs and commuter towns ringing Philadelphia quickly give way to farmlands and nature. It is a region that to this day remains green, vibrant, and—even accounting for recent surges in development—largely unspoiled by the oversaturation of concrete and pavement.

This is the area where Carl Gugasian grew up and spent most of his life. He was born in 1947 in Broomall, a baby boomer in a bedroom community just south of the famously wealthy Main Line, a string of small towns that slide out from Philly's commercial center with historic, old-money names like Lower Merion, Haverford, Bryn Mawr, and Radnor. After a stint in the army and plenty of years in higher ed., Radnor was where Carl Gugasian would come to settle, eventually finding footing in a one-bedroom apartment that belied his net worth: over half a million dollars, every penny of it earned robbing banks.

•

Both of Carl Gugasian's parents were immigrants from Armenia, and they worked hard to give their children what they hadn't had: an easy childhood; the American Dream. As such, though Gugasian didn't grow up rich, he didn't grow up poor, either, which makes it hard to explain why as a teen he decided to try to steal from a neighborhood candy store. Either way, he did it, and he was caught, and at age fifteen, Carl Gugasian was sent to a children's state reformatory. He did his time and got out young enough, but while he was in there, something inside of him broke. It wasn't obvious. Nobody noticed. But it unquestionably changed him forever.

Gugasian ended up going on to Villanova for college, where he studied electrical engineering and joined the ROTC; after fulfilling his mandatory army duty at Fort Bragg, North Carolina, he applied for and received service funding to continue his education, earning a master's degree in systems analysis from the University of Pennsylvania—an Ivy League school—and a doctorate in statistics and probability from Penn State. However, despite all his successes, Gugasian never got a real job.

Why? Because he believed he couldn't.

Call it the impressionability of youth, but all the scared-straight talk Gugasian received in reformatory seemed to have affected him, as intended—just with an unintended effect. "He didn't know that juvenile records get expunged," FBI agent Ray Carr later said. Because of his minor—by both definitions—criminal past, Gugasian "thought he'd never be able to get a real job."

The kid honestly believed that thanks to his one indiscretion, he'd have nothing left to live for no matter what he did. He spent over a decade climbing ever further up the ladder of higher education, which, while to others, seemed like striving for success, to Gugasian felt like delaying the inevitable. So when he reached the top rung and earned his PhD, it didn't spell a triumph. To his mind, it meant only the end of his eligibility to work as a graduate assistant, and the beginning—or rather, the inevitable resumption—of his life of larceny.

This critical lack of understanding aside, Gugasian was undeniably smart. He was methodical, a natural planner, and as his scholastic background would attest, he was preternaturally mathematically inclined. Making calculations was what he'd been taught to do; therefore, he turned robbing a bank into a numbers game. When are banks likely to have the most money on hand? When are there likely to be few customers around? When are bank employees most likely to be tired, distracted, and loath to put up physical resistance? The answer to all these questions was Friday just before closing time, and that's when Gugasian would strike.

Gugasian was a trained systems analyst and a statistician. To him, it was only natural that he would develop a robust, logical system to bank robbery, one that would help him determine which banks to hit, where, when, and how. His methods were successful: they helped him elude detection for three decades, and every choice he made was ingeniously designed to minimize his risk of capture.

Gugasian's m.o. was to first go to the nearby Philadelphia Public Library and scour maps and zoning atlases, looking for small, semi-rural towns with commensurately small police forces. (He began his work in the 1970s, long before the dawn of the internet.) Then he'd try to find banks in those towns built right next to woodland areas, such as state parks. Best of all were parks that, in addition to banks, bordered major highways on another side. Once he identified a target, he scouted it, and once he'd completed his reconnaissance, he struck.

Gugasian wore a Halloween-style mask over his face, custom-adjusted to fit snugly to his skin. That way, no one could see his hair or even positively identify his skin color. He'd work only in colder months, October through April, giving him a reason both inside the banks and out to wear gloves and cover his body in multiple layers of clothes. Not only would this eliminate the chance of leaving any fingerprints, it also made it nearly impossible for anyone to gauge his true weight or body type. He'd also stealthily crouch and slide through the bank lobby rather than run or walk, so no eyewitness could ever provide a clear estimate of his height. Lastly, he liked to jump directly from the floor to the top of the tellers' stand almost immediately after entering. This allowed him both the physical and the mental advantage of the high ground, and the display of athleticism and fitness frequently cowed the tellers into submission and compliance.

He'd hit the cash drawers only, never the vault. In two minutes, he'd be gone: out the door with the money and without a trace.

Gugasian was never captured during a heist. To the cops, it seemed that they just couldn't get there in time—but of course, there was more to it than that. As impressive as his preparations and his regimented process inside the bank were, it was his method of escape that really set him apart from other thieves.

Rather than jump into a getaway car, Gugasian would run straight into the woods. There, hidden, would be a mountain bike, and Gugasian would simply hop on and ride silently away from the scene of the crime via off-road trails. Police cars, driving in from the other direction, along the street, never caught Gugasian. How could they? They were coming from the wrong direction! Within minutes, Gugasian could put miles of distance between himself and the bank he'd just hit, and he'd never cross a cop's path. Eventually, he'd emerge from the far side of the park and reach a waiting, nondescript panel van that he'd parked there hours before. He'd throw the money and the bike in the back, shut the rear doors, then calmly pull out onto the highway without so much as a single eyewitness to the getaway car.

His technique was ingenious. Not only did nobody know how this robber managed to escape every time, no one had any clue who he was.

•

Gugasian was prepared, committed, and smart. He almost never deviated from his script, and he was never caught in the act. He might have never been caught at all, in fact, had it not been for a combination of his inordinate success and a little bit of dumb luck.

One April morning in Radnor, PA, two teenage kids were playing by a culvert in a wooded park. By this point, Gugasian was fifty-three years old, and he'd been robbing banks longer than he hadn't. As the kids poked around, one of them found a three foot long PVC pipe stashed in the soil, capped at both ends. He took it out and opened it, and inside he found schematics, notes, press clippings, maps—and a number of guns.

The kids called the police. The police called the FBI. And for the first time in the nearly three decades of bank robberies perpetrated by this unknown thief—a thief by now dubbed the "Friday Night Bandit" for the time he liked to work—law enforcement officers had a lead as to his identity.

The serial numbers on the recovered guns had all been filed off, so they offered no further information. Many of the documents, however, did. The news clippings and notes all related to banks that had been robbed in the same way, by the same perpetrator, over the past thirty years. One, for instance, listed the name of a bank with the notation "F-7" scratched alongside. It was a bank that had been robbed right near its closing time on a Friday: 7 p.m. There was no question that agents and officers were now on the right track.

The maps were especially helpful: they led investigators to the locations of other, similar caches scattered throughout woodlands across Eastern Pennsylvania. When these caches were unearthed, they yielded similar items, and more: martial arts books. Piles of stolen cash. Halloween masks. And more guns.

Police, ATF, and FBI agents scrutinized the firearms, and they found that though almost all of the guns had been altered and anonymized, one, inexplicably, had not. Tracing its history via a serial number that had been left intact, they found it had been reported stolen from somewhere outside the Fort Bragg area in the early 1970s. Combined with other information—the perpetrator's obvious physical fitness, interest in martial arts, skills with mapmaking, and familiarity with wilderness terrain—leading FBI agent Ray Carr began to craft a likely profile.

The robber had started nearly thirty years ago. Coupled with the fact that he was still active and in great shape, that would mean that he was probably in his mid-fifties—much younger, and he couldn't have committed those first crimes; much older, and he wouldn't be able to continue to work. He'd probably received special training in survival and self-defense; given his clear interest in varied weaponry, he might have received that training in the military—probably while stationed at Fort Bragg. As all of his crimes had been committed alone, he was likely to be an unmarried loner, and given the location of all his stash cites, he probably lived in the suburbs of Philadelphia.

Additionally, it seemed likely that he regularly practiced martial arts, not least because among all the martial arts training books, investigators found a relatively recent flyer for a small chain of martial arts dojos in the Broomall, PA, area. They went to one of the locations and asked the owner if any of his students were very fit, very committed, and middle-aged. The owner offered a list of clients who fit the bill: among them was a third-degree black-belt named Carl Gugasian.

Investigators began to research Gugasian's background, and quickly, all the pieces began to fit into place. He'd been stationed at Fort Bragg, where he'd received special forces training, and he was a bachelor who lived just one block away from the Radnor park where the first cache of clues had been found. Acquaintances said he liked to go jogging in street clothes while weighted down by a heavy backpack—practice runs, it would seem, for his bank jobs. According to his IRS statements, he'd never held down a full-time job; he claimed to be a self-employed statistical analyst and gambler. That was the official explanation for net assets that totaled over $500,000 in cash—all of which, ironically, he kept in the bank.

In short order, police zeroed in. They tailed Gugasian from his home to the Philadelphia Public Library, a trip he made, without question, to plan what would have been his next spate of crimes, and arrested him as he stepped out of his car.

•

By the time he was caught, Carl Gugasian had become the single most prolific bank robber in American history. He hit more banks than John Dillinger, Willie Sutton, or even Bonnie & Clyde. Despite that, he received a sentence of just seventeen and a half years—comparatively light, given his impressive body of work, but reduced for two key reasons: one, Gugasian confessed to his crimes and provided law enforcement officers with all the locations of all his robberies and his hidden stashes, and two, like Frank Abagnale in *Catch Me If You Can*, he agreed to consult with the FBI to improve their training programs designed to help agents track and capture bank robbers.

If Gugasian hadn't been so prolific and so successful, he never would have had to keep so many stash pots for his money and gear, let alone maps to pinpoint all their locations. Of course, if it seems a shame, almost foolish, that Gugasian was brought down largely by the notes and materials he'd felt compelled to save, and in many cases created by his own hand, it shouldn't. The maps, the notes—these weren't the oversights of an otherwise fastidious and careful thief. They were necessary. As Chris Sanchirico, professor of law, business, and public policy at the University of Pennsylvania Law School wrote in his *Stanford Law Review* article about evidence, the creation of such mnemonic assistants was absolutely necessary.

"[W]e litter the world with devices that compensate for our limited cognitive capacity. We make packing lists…we make to-do lists…we buy how-to manuals and save instruction booklets because we cannot figure out how things work on our own…. We scratch out complicated calculations because it is difficult to remember what digit is in the tens place while carrying the two to the top of the thousands column. We supplement our memories with cabinets and hard drives full of files. We back up electronic data because if we lost key documents we would not remember their contents. We label the backups so we can find them later. Largely unnecessary for a hypothetical creature with unlimited cognitive capacity, such devices are essential for the actual creatures that we are…

Carl Gugasian, who depending on one's definition may be the most 'successful' bank robber in US history, was recently convicted precisely by these means. A bachelor's degree in electrical engineering; a master's degree in systems analysis; doctoral work in statistics and probability; native cleverness; a special agility with numbers; training in weapons, survival, self-defense, and map reading with Army Special Forces; uncommon mental and physical discipline—none of this changed the fact that Gugasian could not keep it all in his head."

The surveillance notes of the banks, the maps to the targets and his troves…those were the clues that led to Gugasian's arrest and eventual downfall, yes, but they had to be made. The inability to expect perfect and total recall is quite simply a part of the human condition.

Gugasian, we can only assume, had plenty of time to ponder all of this during his seventeen-plus years in federal custody.

CHAPTER 4

—

Mansfield, TX–David Graham and Diane Zamora

Mansfield, Texas, is a small-town. Sitting in the suburbs south of Fort Worth, itself a smaller sister city to Dallas, it's the kind of place where violent crime long seemed a fairy tale: something that came into the home only on episodes of *Dateline*, to be replaced, once the TV clicked off, by pep rallies, Friday night football games, and meetings of the junior ROTC.

It was an oasis of calm in a turbulent world. It was not the kind of place where anyone expected a girl sneaking out of her house to meet a boy on a school night would be bludgeoned, shot, and left to die in a field in a tangle of barbed wire.

"This does not happen to people last-named Jones in a little town like Mansfield, Texas," said Linda Jones, mother of three, including a sixteen-year-old sophomore named Adrianne. But happen it did, and all because of a young woman's insatiable jealousy and a young man's desperation at letting down his girlfriend.

·

David Graham was the poster child of a good small-town Christian kid, the kind of son that parents everywhere dream of raising. He decided as a youth he wanted to be a pilot, and even as he grew, he kept his goal in his sights. As a twelve-year-old, he joined the

Civil Air Patrol, a kind of proto-air force civilian organization that prepares young people for military careers, and he earned his pilot's license at age fourteen, before he could legally drive. By his senior year in high school, he'd been named the commanding officer of his Civil Air Patrol post, and he even received a commission to attend college at the national Air Force Academy in Colorado, where he planned to begin the path to becoming an officer and, he hoped, fly planes for his country.

Despite not being one of the in-crowd kids, the kind who experiments with drugs and alcohol too early, David Graham was well respected and well liked. He was, as classmate Sarah Layton said, "The perfect guy, the perfect gentleman...one of the last cool guys on earth."

Diane Zamora was a lot like David Graham: they were both driven high schoolers with a future. The oldest of four children, Zamora worked hard. She wanted to be an astronaut, and she pushed herself to earn A's, to take the hardest classes in math and physics, and to study by candlelight if need be when her immigrant parents couldn't find the money to pay the electric bill. She lived a few miles from Mansfield and went to school in a different district, but she too joined the Civil Air Patrol, and that's where she met David Graham.

For quite a while, Zamora and Graham kept one another at arm's length, neither wanting the demands of a significant other to stand between themselves and their goals. However, eventually, their emotions got the better of them, and by the time their senior year rolled around in the late summer of 1995, the two had become a serious item.

"No matter what we were talking about, Diane brought up David's name," said Ronnie Gonzalez, Zamora's cousin. The two quickly became deeply ensconced in one another in that all-consuming way in which young lovers all too often seem to become entangled. Graham's friend Layton also noticed the change. "If you got David away from her and her away from David, they were totally different people. But if you got them together, David was more quiet, and she was more edgy and tense. I don't know if she was wanting to control him or was just insecure… At a point, it seemed almost obsessive."

As the two grew closer, their relationship grew more unhealthily codependent, more dangerous. In short order, they found themselves sacrificing ever more of their values and individual identities to the entity that the two of them had become. David let Diane borrow his truck, an almost unthinkable act for a Texas boy. Predictably, Diane crashed it. Diane, who'd frequently and loudly proclaimed her intent to remain a virgin until marriage, slept with David, leaving her for weeks afterward feeling riddled with guilt.

David began slacking off and lost his command position at his Civil Air Patrol post, but he didn't seem to care. Diane declared she was going to give up both her lifelong dream of becoming an astronaut and the scholarship offers her hard work had earned her, and intended instead to follow David into military service. It was too late to get into the Air Force Academy—she'd missed the application deadline—but she decided she'd apply to the US Naval Academy in Annapolis, and after four years there, she'd simply petition to transfer her commission to a different branch of military.

Their lives turned still more frenetic and illogical. They'd been dating less than three months before they announced to their parents and friends their plans to marry. Conceding that they'd be spending their whole college careers on opposite sides of the country, they set a wedding date nearly five years in the future. Loved ones became nervous about the direction their relationship was headed.

•

And then came Regionals.

In the early morning hours of December 3, 1995, a farmer driving along a desolate country road saw the body of a teenage girl on the ground behind a barbed wire fence. At first, he thought he was looking at road kill. The girl's face was nearly unrecognizable. One bullet hole was in her left cheek, another in her forehead. She had been hit so hard on the left side of her head that the part of the skull above her ear was caved in like a pumpkin. She was wearing flannel shorts and a gray T-shirt that read, "UIL Region I Cross Country Regionals 1995." Within hours, police officers identified her as Adrianne Jones, a sixteen-year-old high school sophomore from the town of Mansfield.

—Skip Hollandsworth, "The Killer Cadets," *Texas Monthly*

•

Fall in Texas is a fine time. The oppressive heat of summer has started to give way, and along with football, cross-country is one of the sports that seems custom made for the season. Cool breezes dapple runners crisscrossing the state's network of trailheads and parks with blessed relief, even as the turning foliage grants access to the kind of unspoiled, natural beauty that evokes a sense of poetics in some.

Student-athletes across the state look forward to the capstone games and meets at the end of their school seasons, and the runners of Mansfield High were no exception. On Friday, November 3rd, the young men and women of Mansfield's cross-country team—the Tigers—drove five hours from their hometown to Lubbock, Texas to compete in their regional championship.

On November 4th, they raced. On November 5th, they drove home.

By November 6th, something had gone very wrong.

Among the members of the Mansfield returning home from regionals satisfied, if not triumphant, was Adrianne Jones, a good-looking blonde who'd been known to spend her Friday evenings sitting in a folding chair on her front lawn with her friends, waiting for boys to drive-up and chat away the time. She did have a boyfriend, but she didn't get to see him as often as she might have liked—her father was relatively strict. She wasn't allowed out past nine, even on weekends, and except for going to school or sports or Golden Fried Chicken, the local fast-food joint where she held down a part time job, she didn't often get to leave the house at all.

She didn't have much chance to be alone with boys, and as a sixteen-year-old girl—one who was pretty, and friendly, and knew it—she certainly couldn't be blamed for wanting to stay in the company of an older, good-looking guy just a little bit longer. So when all the Mansfield Tigers piled out of the van after returning home from Lubbock, Adrianne asked David Graham for a ride home. And when he agreed, she had him take a couple of intentionally wrong turns, until they ended up parked behind the local elementary school.

What happened next remains surprisingly unclear, but what is for certain is that about a month later, when David Graham broke down crying and told his girlfriend that he'd had sex with Adrianne Jones.

It's interesting. When she had been single, had she been asked what she would have done if a boyfriend cheated on her, Diane Zamora would unquestionably have said that she would have broken up with him on the spot. But that's not what she did with David Graham, nor did she ask for an apology. She didn't say she needed time to think about it, and she didn't decide to go out and have a fling of her own.

Instead, she forgave him—but only to a point. She told David Graham that their love had been sullied, and if he wanted to save it, it had to be "purified."

To go forward, the stain on their relationship had to be cleansed. The sin had to be erased.

On the night of December 3rd, as she drove home with her mother from a nearby gym, Adrianne Jones declared that she knew what she wanted to do when she grew up: she wanted to become a behavioral scientist. "I want to figure out what makes people act the way they do," she said.

Less than four hours later, she'd be dead.

•

Most of the evidence suggests that the plan was Zamora's, but that doesn't excuse Graham. Zamora brought the righteous fury, but Graham willingly supplied his muscle.

On the night of December 3rd—late at night, after she'd made it home from the gym and after her mother had already told her daughter to go to bed—Adrianne Jones received a call from David Graham. He asked her to see her, asked her to sneak out of the house once everyone else had gone asleep, and telling no one, she agreed.

David was driving Diane's Mazda hatchback. Adrianne didn't think anything of it; he was driving borrowed cars all the time, since Diane had wrecked his truck. But unbeknownst to Adrianne, Diane was in the car—she was hiding in the back. And she'd convinced David to pick up Adrianne, drive her somewhere secluded, and when they parked, let Diane jump out of the back and smash in Adrianne's head in with a dumbbell weight. If that didn't kill her, David would finish the job by strangling her or snapping her neck, whereupon they'd tie her body down with the weight and dispose of Adrianne's body.

The first part of the plan worked fine. Adrianne slipped out of her house and into David's waiting car, and the two of them— three, counting the stowaway in the back—drove out toward Joe Pool Lake. When they arrived, Diane leapt out of the back, iron dumbbell weight in hand, and bashed Adrianne in the head.

The only problem was that Adrianne didn't die. As David would later testify, Adrianne escaped, shaking free of Diane's and David's attempts to hold her down and crawling out the window. However, she didn't get far: the blow from the weight had shattered her skull, and she was barely able to walk. She stumbled out into the darkness, then got caught up in a barbed wire fence, all but unable to move.

"She's dead," David said. But Diane insisted she wasn't. So David took his pistol, which he always carried, and fired two rounds into Adrianne's head, a pair of thunderclaps that split the night.

His military training served him well. His aim was excellent: one of the shots penetrated the front of her brain, exiting right between the eyes.

The girl was dead. The stain on their relationship, such as it was, had been cleansed. But before David even managed to return to the car, the gravity of what they'd done had taken hold of them.

"We shouldn't have done that," Diane would say, examining the bloodstains in her car and on her clothes.

"Now you tell me," David mused, though it was of course far too late. They ditched their clothes. They tried to act normally, pull it back together. And they each promised one another that they'd never tell anybody what they'd done.

It was not a promise they would keep.

•

Linda Jones knew something was wrong the moment she woke up. The alarm in her daughter's bedroom was ringing, and it wouldn't shut off.

When she went in to check, she found Adrianne's bed made and empty, and her daughter was nowhere in sight. At first, she thought Adrianne might have gone for a morning jog, but then her son pointed out that Adrianne's running shoes were still sitting on the floor.

Linda called the school. Office staff told her that Adrianne had not come in, that she was absent.

That's when Linda called the police. To hear her tell it, she already knew. It was only a matter of time to remove all doubt.

Her daughter's body was found that morning and identified that afternoon; by evening, it had been confirmed. Adrianne Jones was dead.

The town fell into mourning. This was not the kind of thing that happened. Sheriffs began investigating in earnest. There was trauma to her head and there were gunshot wounds, but there were no signs of rope burns or residue around her wrists or ankles. This had not, it seemed, been an abduction. Similarly, there was no evidence of sexual assault, so this was not a murder tied to a rape. Adrianne had a history of sneaking out of after curfew—her mother had even taken to nailing her windows shut to try to discourage the scheme—so investigators concluded that in all likelihood, she'd left the house willingly before she'd met her end.

That meant that the killer was, almost definitely, somebody Adrianne knew.

The police interviewed countless potential suspects and persons of interest, but no leads seemed to go anywhere. Adrianne's boyfriend had an alibi. So did a girl who'd assaulted one of Adrianne's friends with a baseball bat a few years prior. Even a young depressive who'd worked at a pharmacy near the Subway where Adrianne had once part-timed—and had freaked her out by his constant visits and ploys to get her attention—was questioned and held, but then cleared.

In time, the trail ran cold, and authorities dialed down their efforts. Adrianne's school did plant a tree for her near the soccer field, but that was cold comfort for friends and family who were left with nothing but questions that seemed to have no answers. As the academic year drew toward a close, Mansfield High decided to dedicate its annual yearbook to her as well. That, unfortunately, seemed as though it would be the end of things. It very nearly was, too, and the matter was given up for lost, until the following fall when investigators were contacted by an unexpected source: a military investigator calling all the way from Maryland with information about an unsolved murder.

•

When they still lived down the road from one another, it all sounded so easy. In the real world, however, Maryland and Colorado are quite far apart, and for two teenage kids who'd never been more than a few miles away from one another, multiple time zones and the burdens of being new recruits to military life began to take their toll. Even with email, the lack of constant physical contact made it easy for the two to start feeling far, far removed from one another.

Diane Zamora was the first to break. As she had with David Graham in the Civil Air Patrol, she found herself developing feelings for her squad leader, an upperclassman named Jay Guild. It started with confiding in Guild her troubles—missing her boyfriend, feeling abandoned and lonely when he didn't answer her emails quickly enough. She started having crying jags, and she told Guild that she feared that David was cheating on her, even as Zamora drew even closer. She kissed Guild, and she tried to convince him that despite military protocol and the existence of her own boyfriend across the country, perhaps the two of them should date. But Guild resisted. He was fine being friends and nothing more, and besides, he could tell something just wasn't right. Beyond the fact that Zamora talked so often of David Graham that she was clearly still devoted to him, she also told Guild matter-of-factly that she'd previously killed a rival for his attentions—and would kill again if need be. He didn't believe her, but kind of talk was still enough of red flag to keep anyone's emotions in check.

As he would testify in court a year later, "She had told me one time that she had promised David that if she had ever cheated on him, that she would do the same thing for him that they had already done."

The prosecutor clarified, "She would kill the person that she cheated with?"

Replied Guild, "Yes."

Incredibly, her squad leader wasn't the only person to whom Zamora divulged the crime she'd committed, the one she and David Graham had sworn to never confess to a soul. In a late-night conversation with her roommates, Zamora offered something between an admission and outright bragging about what she and David had done. They were talking about love, they were talking about the worst things they'd ever done—and then, all of a sudden, Diane Zamora was telling her new roommates, girls that she'd known for less than sixty days, everything that had happened out at Joe Pool Lake.

Unlike Guild, they believed her.

The next morning, they talked to a Navy chaplain. The chaplain told a naval attorney. And soon after that, detectives from a small Texas town found themselves boarding a plane for Annapolis.

A few days later, those detectives also flew to Colorado Springs.

•

The trials were short. Both Graham and Zamora pled not guilty, despite the fact that both of them offered written confessions shortly after having been brought into custody. Though each confession was written independently, each mirrored the other in its details. What's more, they also left copious physical evidence that removed all doubt. Diane's senior year date planner showed an entry for December 4th: a circle and an arrow leading to a note that read, "Adrianne: 1:38 AM." Adrianne's blood was also found in the upholstery of Diane's car, and David willingly led investigators to the spot in his parents' attic where he'd hidden the killing tools after the fact: the dumbbell weights and the pistol.

Adrianne's parents' asking prosecutors to refrain from seeking capital punishment was the only thing that spared them the death penalty.

As horrible as it is to say, these kind of things happen all the time. Love triangles are illogical and dumb, but sometimes, people do get murdered. The simple fact that these two teenagers conspired to kill another high schooler isn't what makes them so pitiable, so cruel. What makes them so rank, so bad, is the fact that this crime didn't have to happen—and not just in the rhetorical sense. It *truly* didn't have to happen, as in, there was just no reason for it.

Because in truth, David Graham never had sex with Adrianne Jones at all.

.

In a televised interview years after his conviction, David Graham admitted the following:

> In my statement I said that I had had sex with Adrianne. I have recanted that statement, and what I said in that statement wasn't true.
> Never did I imagine the heartache it would cause…I just shut it all out of my mind that instant when I convinced myself that Diane was even worth murder. After Diane gave me the ultimatum, I thought long and hard about how to carry out the crime. I was stupid, but I was in love.

At David Graham's trial, both the defense and the prosecution attorneys agreed that David had never actually had sex with Adrianne Jones. If that's the case, it begs the question: why did David go through with it? Why didn't he just come clean? Even if he had initially lied to Zamora, whatever his reasons—to get a rise out of her, to test her devotion, to attempt to end the relationship—when he saw the road that it was taking him down, why didn't he simply tell Diane the truth?

Or as Adrianne Jones' father David asked when he saw Graham's face on TV during the trials, "What kind of a spineless asshole are you?"

It is, perhaps the worst part—knowing that even as senseless as the taking of life can be, this was especially so.

In examining just how bad a person can become, David Graham and Diane Zamora can't be separated. Neither is worse than the other. Each are equally bad.

Their obsessions fed upon one another's, and together they committed the worst of crimes, its utter vileness compounded by just how unnecessary it all was. She was dramatically manipulative and passionately jealous, and he was happy to go to any lengths to stand close to her flame.

The two never did marry, as it turned out. Their last words to one another were, "I love you," before receiving life sentences with a minimum of forty years in jail before the possibility of parole.

Seven years into her sentence, Diane Zamora wed another inmate, an arsonist with whom she had corresponded by mail. The two had never met.

CHAPTER 5

—

Bath Township, MI—
Andrew Kehoe

The twentieth century was brought to a close by one of the most tragic events in American public life: the Columbine shootings. Perpetrated by high schoolers Eric Harris and Dylan Klebold, the Columbine shootings led to the deaths of fifteen people and are considered by many, especially among those born into Generations X and Y, to be the progenitor of the school massacre.

Certainly, mass killings have unfortunately woven themselves into the fabric of American life since then, particularly in public places such as schools. Recent killings at Sandy Hook Elementary and Virginia Tech come quickly to mind. However, Columbine was neither the deadliest nor the first mass school shooting in the USA. Long before Columbine, a former US Marine armed himself with a sniper rifle, climbed the University of Texas clock tower on a summer day in 1966 and rained bullets upon the city of Austin for over an hour and a half. And yet, even that assault, deadly as it was, paled in comparison to America's first and worst school killings: the 1927 Bath Massacre, perpetrated by Andrew Kehoe.

Few, if any, survivors of the Bath Massacre remain, and perhaps that, coupled with the fact that the event took place in the days before the ubiquity of television news and constant coverage, may have helped its perpetrator slip away into the relative anonymity of time. However, there is no denying that Andrew Kehoe carried out the single most destructive school killing in America's history, bringing death to forty-five people and permanent, disfiguring injury to dozens more.

And it all started over property taxes.

•

Andrew Kehoe had never been a giving man. He was far from charitable, and he was certainly not one to ever put another's needs before his own. In fact, he was an egotist of the worst kind, the kind of person who fails to recognize not only that other people also have hopes and desires, but that those hopes and desires even have a right to exist.

It's said that when he prepared to sell off some familial ranch land early in his life, he visited his neighbor and hawked off all his property's firewood—selling it for next to nothing—just before closing the deal. When asked why he would do such a thing, he replied that he didn't want the new owner to get anything he hadn't explicitly paid for.

Kehoe was exactly the kind of man who would happily cut off his nose to spite his face, if he thought the nose had done him wrong. He would also, it turned out, be willing to do quite a whole lot more.

Bath Township is a central Michigan suburb just north of East Lansing. East Lansing, sister city to the capital, was where Kehoe attended college at Michigan State, where he majored in electrical engineering, and where he met a wealthy young girl named Nellie Price, the woman who would soon become his wife. In 1919, after

Kehoe and Price married, the two purchased a plot of farmland from Price's aunt and uncle for $12,000. Kehoe paid his in-laws $6,000 in cash, and he took out a $6,000 mortgage for the rest.

Kehoe loved tinkering, tools, and technology—his electrical engineering degree spoke to as much. He wasn't much of a farmer, though, nor much of a businessman, and despite his knack for fine-tuning his tractors to try to maximize his farm's yield, he couldn't seem to turn a profit. He began to spend as much energy complaining he'd overpaid for his land and trying to wriggle out of his debt as he did tilling his soil.

True, all farmers were forced to contend with plummeting wholesale prices for crops throughout the 1920s, but it certainly didn't hurt that Kehoe had no love at all for nature. For starters, he couldn't stand to be unclean; by neighbors' accounts, as soon as he got dirty, he insisted upon dropping whatever he was doing, going home to wash, then changing his clothes before returning to his work. Tough standards for a working farmer. Additionally, Kehoe had no touch whatsoever with animals. He shot a neighbor's dog for barking, he fed a newly-purchased cow wet clover until it developed a bloated stomach and died, and he even beat his own workhorse to death for plowing too slowly. Clearly, his own ineptitude didn't make managing operations any easier.

Though Kehoe failed at running his own farm, he did succeed elsewhere in Bath: as a campaigner. In 1922, three years after Kehoe married and settled onto his parcel of land, Bath Township replaced its chain of scattershot one-room schoolhouses with a single, consolidated school. Many hailed what was then seen as a progressive step: busing students to a central location to divide them into classrooms by grade would allow for better facilities and a better education.

Kehoe, however, was infuriated. A new central school meant construction of a new school building, and to Andrew Kehoe, a new municipal building meant only one thing: taxes.

Everyone in Bath saw their property taxes jump in 1922, 1923, and 1924. Many grumbled, but Kehoe felt the increased assessments as a personal slight. The concepts of payment, ownership, and debt always held outside influence to Kehoe. There had been the incident with the firewood, yes, but it ran deeper than that. Kehoe had been raised Roman Catholic, as had his wife Nellie, and his whole life, they had been devout churchgoers. However, that all came to an end when their parish decided to consecrate a new church, and their priest asked Kehoe to tithe four hundred dollars to aid in its construction.

From that day forward, Kehoe never attended church services again. He didn't let his wife go, either.

Kehoe was just the kind of narcissist who felt all he'd touched was his, that he owed nothing to either the community or the world. Powered by his self-righteous anger, he railed so vehemently against the increased property taxes that he got himself nominated and elected to the school board, all under the banner of curtailing spending.

Which to Kehoe meant, as best as possible, cutting it off entirely.

Quickly, Kehoe became both the school board's treasurer and its obstructionist voice. Anything that needed to be done, if it involved spending money, he voted against it. In short order, he began to lose friends and influence in the town as he attempted to quash even the smallest of school expenditures—even paying the bus drivers. He held in particular disdain the school superintendent, E. E. Huyck, whose uselessness and expendability he'd constantly proclaim. While his neighbors had appreciated his zeal for pulling back from unnecessary expenditures, they grew to fear his combativeness, as he refused to compromise and went so far as to move immediately adjourn any board meeting he felt he wasn't going his way.

Emboldened by his position of power on the school board, Kehoe ran for town clerk in 1926. To no one's great surprise but his own, he was defeated. And thereafter, something in him seemed to change. He wasn't far off.

Come late 1926, Kehoe's neighbor Monty Ellsworth noted that Kehoe's farm had stopped growing anything. When it came time to harvest wheat, there was nothing for Kehoe to do. A man to whom Kehoe had given a horse even returned it, half-fearing that Kehoe might be ridding himself of possessions en route to committing suicide.

Kehoe very nearly might have receded from Bath Township society altogether, were it not for one thing. That summer, the new school had become infested by a swarm of bees. Huyck, the superintendent, was tasked with the job of removing the infestation, but he failed. Kehoe, reveling in pointing out the shortcomings of the man he'd come to see as his rival, volunteered to take care of the job himself. When he succeeded in ridding the school of pests, he volunteered to become the school's general caretaker and custodian, an offer that was swiftly accepted.

Nobody, then, thought it was odd that Kehoe began spending so much time at the school the following year, particularly in the basements and tunnels underneath it. No one considered that it might be anything but goodwill that drove Kehoe into the foundations, the exposed underbelly, of the very building that in his mind had come to symbolize everything that he'd grown to hate. And nobody knew that something so minor as failing to win a small-town election could so deeply twist the mind of a man who thought all he saw throughout the world should rightfully be his own.

•

As it happened, there was a lot that people didn't know about Andrew Kehoe. Or, more accurately, there were gaps in their knowledge of him. They did know he was a whiz with electrical systems and wiring, but they didn't know how he came to know as much as he did about explosives. He did know plenty, though, and of that, everyone was aware. In the years before 1927, Kehoe had begun experimenting with explosives in many ways—but positive ways, fruitful ways. Neighborly ways. He blew up tree stumps and rocks for himself and for other farmers who needed them removed in order to better plow their fields. He captained a New Year's Eve explosives show that wowed people throughout the town. He even bought hundreds of pounds of explosives on a trip into Lansing and carried them back to Bath himself, storing them at his farm so that if anyone needed any, they could just visit his place rather than have to trek all the way into the city to be able to pick them up.

Perhaps some assumed that he'd learned about the utility of controlled explosions from farming, or during his college days. But in fact, Andrew Kehoe had known all about the power of bursts of flame for far, far longer.

Andrew Kehoe came from a large family. He was among the youngest of thirteen children, often unsupervised and rarely regarded, and when he was still young—somewhere between five and eight years old—his mother died, stealing from the boy his one source of comfort in a frenetic household. Kehoe's father remarried, which angered Kehoe, not only because he saw it as a betrayal, but because young Andrew Kehoe and his stepmother did not get along. They quarreled, sometimes quite bitterly, and as the years went on, their relationship only grew worse.

On one occasion by the time he'd reached fourteen—perhaps as punishment—Kehoe's stepmother made him stay at home and watch the few remaining younger children while she left for the day to run errands. He was left there, unsupervised, to his own devices. When she returned at day's end, she put away her purchases and began her preparations to cook supper. The next thing she knew, the kitchen's oil-burning stove exploded, bathing her instantly in flaming cooking fuel.

As she burned, Andrew Kehoe watched. Eventually, he threw water on her, which only served to exacerbate the grease fire.

His stepmother died of the injuries she sustained. Shortly thereafter, Andrew Kehoe left to make his way in the world.

Later examination showed the stove had been tampered with.

•

May is generally beautiful in Michigan. Winter has broken and spring is in full bloom, and the sun seems to bathe the world in light. The May of 1927 was no different from those before it. The green smell of growth was in the air. Young students prepared to finish their school years and return home for the summer planting season. And no one thought it odd that the once-quarrelsome Andrew Kehoe seemed to have calmed down.

The signs were all there, perhaps—people simply missed them. At a board meeting, Kehoe uncharacteristically voted to approve all the expenditure bills presented, a knowing grin painted upon his face. A young kindergarten teacher asked Kehoe if she might make use of his woodlands for a school picnic. He agreed, but suggested she moved the date forward—"If you are going to have a picnic," he said, "you would best have it right away." He even playfully ribbed a school bus driver named Warden Keyes, son of one of Kehoe's fellow school board members, when the driver accidentally dropped his paycheck in the mud upon accepting it from Kehoe.

"You want to take good care of that check," Kehoe reportedly said. "It's probably the last check you'll ever get."

Still, nobody could have seen it coming.

On Sunday, May 15th, he rested. Then, for the next two days after the Sabbath, Andrew Kehoe set himself hard to work. First, he went to every tree on his property, stripping each of bark in a circular ring around its base, a process he knew would kill them. Then, he murdered his wife, stashing her body behind the barn.

Next, he spent a fair bit of time meticulously hand-carving and sanding a wooden sign, which he strung to the barbed wire fence at the edge of his property.

He then went to sleep, woke up, had a nice breakfast, and blew up his farm.

It was May 18th, 1927, a Wednesday morning, when Kehoe's property burst into flames. His neighbors saw the conflagration and headed directly over to help—but as they made their way there, they ran across Kehoe going the opposite direction. He waved them off.

"Don't go in there," he said. "Go down to the school."

Turns out, Kehoe's house wasn't the only thing he'd blown up. And his wife wasn't the only one he'd killed.

•

Andrew Kehoe arrived to find the Bath Consolidated School building half blown to high heaven, and it saddened him deeply—principally, the "half" part. The north wing—the side that housed the youngest students, aged seven to twelve—had been completely destroyed, exploded from the ground up with five hundred pounds of military-surplus pyrotol.

As it happened—though nobody yet knew it; they were too busy fighting the resultant fires and combing through the wreckage for survivors—the south wing, which was undamaged, had been wired with explosives, too. Kehoe was apoplectic (although onlookers may have misunderstood why); either the wiring had been laid incorrectly, or it had short circuited, or perhaps something had been knocked asunder from the force of the north wing's blow. Regardless, the city was in bedlam. Nearly forty were dead: mostly children, some teachers. Red Cross workers struggled tirelessly. A local pharmacy became a stand-in trauma ward. Firefighters and farmers pitched in as equals to help.

Of course, Kehoe didn't join in. He just watched the school burn, half admiring his handiwork and half cursing his bad luck...when whom should he see rushing to the scene than the man he hated more than any: the school superintendent, E. E. Huyck.

Kehoe couldn't believe his bad luck in failing to kill Huyck with the blast. However, he didn't lament it too long. He had a contingency in place.

He had his rifle. He called Huyck over to his car. And when Huyck approached, Kehoe aimed his weapon—not at Huyck, but at his trunk, where he'd stashed another hundred or so pounds of explosives.

Then, he fired off his final round.

For years in Bath—decades, a generation—disfigured people stalked the town. Those who grew up there didn't ask why; everyone knew. It wasn't that they came home injured from WWII, a Purple Heart resting on their mantelpiece. It was that they'd had half their face sheared off, or a femoral artery pierced, or an eye gouged out when Andrew Kehoe blew up the schoolhouse, and they'd lived their whole lives crippled. Disfigured. Maimed.

And they were the lucky ones.

The coroner's inquest was long, but the findings were fast in coming. As an act of revenge against all he'd felt had done him wrong—his wife and her family for necessitating the loan on the farm, the town for voting him out of office, the superintendent and even the children themselves for being the source of those goddamn taxes to begin with—Andrew Kehoe killed as many people as he could in the best way he knew how. In the manner he'd already known would succeed.

The worst part? He really needn't have.

By post-mortem estimates, Andrew Kehoe had amassed so many tools in his time at the farm that if he'd simply sold them, he could have easily paid off his loan outright, and then some. However, it seemed he simply didn't want to. To Kehoe's mind, those were his, just as the farm should have been rightfully his. He was like a kid with his toys: if he couldn't have something, he didn't want anyone else to have them, either.

It was true with the trees, and it was true with everything else, too. When investigators came, they found more than just Kehoe's wife's remains in the wreckage of the barn—they found Kehoe's animals, too. He'd locked them all up to ensure they'd perish as well. His wife's family, the ones who'd sold him the land, stood to re-inherit the farm once Andrew Kehoe and Nellie Price had passed, and Kehoe wanted to make sure that what they got was worth as little as possible.

Kehoe's neighbors had known he'd stopped growing crops. What they hadn't known was that he'd stopped paying his mortgage tax, too—as well as his insurance. After the rubble was cleared and damages paid, his former in-laws found themselves left with nothing.

The town of Bath was never the same, not for years after Kehoe committed his crimes. Ronald Bauerle, great-nephew of one of the victims, says he remembers one of his old family members telling him that for years after, Michigander children not even alive at the time of the blast would offer prayers at night before going to bed, offering "love to everybody in the world, except Kehoe."

A series of memorials commemorating the victims of the Bath School bombing is all that remains at the site of the worst school killing in America. All that stands now is a cupola of remembrance and a sign, a plaque that lists the names of the dead.

There was the other sign too, of course. The one that Kehoe himself made and hung on his barbed wire fence as he finally committed the barbarous act he'd spent a whole school year planning.

"Criminals are made, not born," it read.

It flapped in the wind for days until somebody finally took it down.

CHAPTER 6

—

Mountain City, TN—
Jenelle Potter

Mountain City, Tennessee, is a small, country town in the Appalachian mountain range, nestled deep inside Cherokee National Forest. Its primary homegrown business is a gas station-slash-restaurant-slash-general store, and besides that, there just isn't much else there. It's thirty miles to the nearest movie theater or bagel place, and a solid two and a half hours to anything resembling a big city. It kisses up against the borders of North Carolina and Virginia, and about 2,500 people live there—that's all.

In short, it's the kind of place where everybody literally knows everybody else, and even in the twenty-first century, nobody bothers to lock their doors. Besides the occasional DWI or fight outside a roadhouse, nothing much ever happens. It's a calm town, quiet, peaceful.

Or at least, it was until the early morning hours of January 31, 2012, when Marvin "Buddy" Potter and Jamie Curd broke into a neighbor's home and executed Bill Payne Jr. and his girlfriend, Billie Jean Hayworth.

Hours passed before their bodies were discovered. Each had been shot once in the head. Their seven month-old boy, Tyler, though physically unharmed, was found trapped in the loving arms of his mother's still-warm corpse.

The scene, unfortunately, left no clues to suspects or a motive. Nothing had been taken from the Payne household; there were no signs of a robbery, a drug deal, or a scuffle. And of course, the baby had been left unharmed. Still, by the next day, Potter and Curd had been charged with the crime, and when confronted, they readily confessed.

They'd done it, yes, but for a reason. They'd felt like they had no choice.

"When you hear people plotting to take your—cut your daughter in a restroom and take her out the back of the store, and they want to take her...in a field and murder her..." Buddy Potter droned during his interrogation, tears at the edges of his eyes. What else was he to do?

His daughter Jenelle was in trouble. He knew as much. There was a $3,000 bounty on her head; he knew that, too. He'd learned from a family friend in the CIA that Bill Payne and Billie Jean Hayworth were plotting to kill his daughter. So what choice did he have? He enlisted Jenelle's boyfriend Jamie, and together, they killed Bill and Billie Jean to protect Jenelle. It was a father's duty. It had to be done.

There was just one problem: Buddy Potter didn't actually know anyone in the CIA. Not anybody real, anyway. And the deeper investigators dug, the more they came to realize the horrible truth: every aspect of the crime—except the brutal murders, that is—was a figment of Jenelle Potter's imagination.

•

Jenelle Potter was born with an auditory processing disorder. Her hearing impairment was severe enough that it eventually led to cognitive problems, which themselves proceeded to limit her mental development and cap her functions of higher learning. She read fine and could speak eruditely, if in an odd sing-song lilt, but her spelling wasn't very good, and she faced limits on her ability to parse non-literal meaning, vocal inflection, and conversational norms. For instance, she didn't understand sarcasm, she often tried to hug people she barely knew, and she had trouble interpreting anything short of unconditional approval as anything other than a direct threat.

"She doesn't understand common joking," Jenelle's older sister Christie told a county prosecutor. Christie also claimed that Jenelle had a history of manipulating her parents, learning from a young age that if she pretended that she needed their help or couldn't do something, then they would do it for her. After they'd left, she'd giggle with glee.

At first, such special treatment seemed to Jenelle to be a positive, but as Jenelle grew older, she found herself trapped in a sheltered, pre-scripted life. Her sister Christie earned an associate's degree, married, and moved away. But Jenelle didn't, and by the time she hit thirty, she found herself still living at home with her parents.

She didn't have a driver's license, so anywhere she wanted to go, her parents had to take her. She had diabetes. She wasn't allowed to have a boyfriend. She was still a virgin, and not by choice. In short, her life was empty, boring, and cold.

Until two things happened: one, she found the internet. And two, she met a man.

As for the internet, it was a beacon of light. Finally, Jenelle had people to talk to, people who didn't judge her on her social oddities or the physical ungainliness of her six-foot frame. Plus, it was a realm in which her parents—older people, not technologically inclined—couldn't keep her constrained.

Secondly, there was the man. Actually, there were two. A pharmacist at a local store who'd taken pity on lonely Jenelle introduced her to two men: the pharmacist's brother, Bill Payne, and their cousin, Jamie Curd.

Bill was a social butterfly. Curd was a computer nerd who'd never had a girlfriend. Payne was the one Potter fell for. Curd was the one she ended up with.

•

"I know Billie that Bitch has lived [with] more guys
and had sex with 80% of Mtn. City."
—Topix.com post, 2011.

•

For a time, Jenelle's life was looking up. Though she had to keep her blossoming relationship with Jamie Curd a secret from her parents, she reveled in having someone special in her life. Unbeknownst to Jenelle's parents, Curd bought her a cell phone. They spoke on it for hours every night, and Jenelle used it to send Jamie nude photographs, a stand-in for intimacy even when they couldn't be physically proximate.

However, Jenelle never lost her crush on Bill Payne. And when he started getting serious with Billie Jean Hayworth, that's when the trouble began.

First, there were the harassing phone calls—ten, twenty calls a day of heavy breathing and hanging up. Next came message board posts like the one above, accusing Billie Jean and her friends of rampant promiscuity and claiming that they all carried HIV. The posts were written under pseudonyms—Matt Potter, Dan White, etc.—but in every case, authored by Jenelle. Jenelle reveled in the anonymity of the internet, and she began creating entire threads of back-and-forth conversations under multiple personae, all decrying the one who'd claimed the object of her affection.

After a while, that wasn't enough. She began posting nasty messages to her own Facebook page, then claimed that she had been "hacked" by Billie Jean and her cabal of mean girls. She started claiming that she herself was the victim of harassment, and not the other way around.

Her parents, technologically unsophisticated as they were, believed every word.

It was right around then that Chris came into the picture.

•

About a year before Jenelle's boyfriend and father took the lives of Bill and Billie Jean, Jenelle's mother Barbara began to get emails from a mysterious man named Chris. In time, Jamie began to receive notes and text messages from him, too. Interestingly, as Tennessee prosecutor Dennis Brooks would later point out, "Chris wrote to Jamie and Barbara through Jenelle's email address.

Apparently, he also had access to Jenelle's Facebook account, where he could further converse with Barbara. He never used any online account of his own. Always Jenelle's."

The claims this "Chris" made were ludicrous. An early letter—again, sent directly from Jenelle's email account—read, verbatim, "I guess you are wondering what my Job is for the CIA and also ICE overseas...I just KILL and I Enjoy that a lot. I get to shoot all the bad guys. And with NICS well I work with some marines over sea's and do things with them and also go on walks and know what's going on there."

Reading this, it seems that anybody with a modicum of sense would immediately recognize this as a falsehood, a fabrication of a fertile but unrefined mind. After all, what is more likely: that there existed an agent of the CIA—a foreign intelligence service—who would not only be posted in a tiny stateside town like Mountain City but also be completely unable to competently spell? Or that this this purported agent, whom no one had ever met in person and who communicated solely through a housebound woman's internet services, was simply the figment of that lonely woman's imagination?

Despite all odds, three people did believe in Chris' existence: Barbara Potter, Buddy Potter, and Jamie Curd. Or perhaps it was just that they wanted to. After all, his life seemed interesting, important, dangerous, and exciting—none of which are words normally used to describe Mountain City. So despite the fact that this Chris appeared to spend his entire career protecting Jenelle Potter and trailing her "enemies," every claim he made—from his corroborations of Jenelle's accusations to his support of Jenelle's increasingly paranoid complaints that there were people "out to get her"—they swallowed hook, line, and sinker.

In short, they had been catfished. It happens all the time: an internet predator cons a target, usually suckering them out of money or coaxing them into a phony amorous relationship. But this time, the targets were manipulated into something far more heinous: murder. And the person pulling the strings was just an envious, lonely girl, who saw nothing wrong with luring her loved ones into executing the people who represented all she wanted but couldn't have.

Throughout the course of a year, Buddy, Jamie, and Barbara were prepped. And when "Chris" told Jenelle's nearest and dearest that she was in grave danger, and that he'd use the CIA's power to shield Buddy and Jamie if they did what had to be done, they believed him.

And they acted.

•

At 6:00 a.m. on January 31, 2012, Buddy Potter and Jamie Curd sat in Buddy's truck a few hundred yards from Bill Payne Jr.'s house. They watched Bill Payne Sr. leave for work, and then they crept forward. They slid open the glass side door, and Jamie Curd stood guard as his girlfriend's father executed both his cousin and his cousin's girlfriend, mother to his cousin's baby.

He threw up afterwards. Then he went home.

That night, he spoke to Jenelle: it had been done. They were safe.

He was brought in for questioning the very next day. In a town as small as Mountain City, everybody really does know everybody else, and prosecutors weren't surprised when Curd confessed to being an accessory to the crime. The only surprise came from the unusual question he asked of the deputies: was anyone from the CIA present at the sheriff's station? That clue was the break investigators needed to put the whole case together.

When he realized the extent of what he had done and how he had been used, Jamie Curd turned state's witness, testifying against the Potters in exchange for plea bargain deal of twenty-five years in prison.

Buddy Potter was charged and successfully convicted of two counts of first-degree murder for executing Bill Payne and Billie Jean Hayworth. His wife, Barbara, was tried and convicted, too, as was Jenelle.

Jenelle Potter, who set in motion all that followed without ever leaving her keyboard, was sentenced to serve two concurrent life terms in the Tennessee Prison for Women.

As a condition of her incarceration, she will not be permitted to access the internet.

CHAPTER 7

—

Evan

I said a few chapters back that *two* more kids from my high school class died since I started writing this book—but so far, I've only written about one.

I mentioned Nick. I did know Nick, but we weren't close. He was a person I recognized, but not someone close to me.

The other person to die was Evan. Evan was different. Evan was a friend. For a while at that idyllic high school of mine, he might have been one of my best friends.

Actually, Evan was one of my first friends back then, and one of the few people I remained close to throughout my time there. When I transferred in from a different junior high, I didn't know more than a handful of kids in my new class. He was one of the first people to reach out and make me feel welcome, to make me feel like I had a place.

And now, he's dead, too.

·

Evan and I met in eighth grade. We had a lot in common, or at least enough. We were nerds: dateless, awkward. We both scored high in class and on tests, but true to the stereotype, we were both socially inept.

We watched cartoons, in a time well before that hit the mainstream for American high school kids. We passed lunch periods in the library playing chess, and after school and on weekends, we got together in living rooms and basements for marathon sessions of Magic: The Gathering. We didn't go to the mall to flirt with girls.

Interestingly, our friendship almost ended as soon as it began. The first year we knew each other, we got into a fight—a physical fight, over an experiment for a science fair.

Think about that—how nerdy a pair of kids has to be to draw blood over homework done for extra credit.

I remember it so clearly: we were in the basement of his parents' house, laying on our stomachs on the beige carpet, drawing charts on posterboard. He didn't like how I was sketching the graph we were trying to make, so he held me down and started twisting my ankle. I swung out at him, my pencil still in hand.

I ended up stabbing him in the back with the #2 lead.

He ran off crying.

Another guy was down there with us—the one who died of the heart defect, actually. I remember us locking eyes, scared at what had just happened.

Ten seconds later, Evan's dad came storming down the stairs, screaming at me inches from my nose as his face flushed red.

I was thirteen, maybe twelve. I thought he was going to beat my ass.

He didn't. However, that marked the end of our project.

We did not win the science fair.

In most houses, I probably would have been unwelcome forever after that. But I wasn't. Evan's dad, like Evan himself, forgave and forgot, and Evan and I grew very close. Throughout the rest of high school, we had almost all our classes together. As we got older and started finding ourselves, we even surfed between social groups together—joining the track team and befriending the athletes, joining plays and befriending the theater kids, joining the alternative education program and befriending the hippie teachers still riding the wave of educational liberalism that had reached a high water mark back in the 1960s and '70s but never fully receded.

Once we got our driver's licenses, we went on road trips together. In the summers, we drove to the beach, and we waited in line to buy tickets to concerts. He was a guy whose phone number I surely knew by heart, back before cell phones made that kind of thing obsolete.

And now, like I said, he's dead.

•

Let's get this out of the way right away: Evan was an idiot. I mean that in the most endearing way possible. He was incredibly intelligent, just goofy, and proud of it. Despite the brain he had on him, he was socially clueless—desperately so. He would, for instance, bust out into song lyrics the middle of math class, not because he thought it would get a laugh, but because he just felt like singing during school. He wore neon and pleather pants and velour shirts, well before irony in clothing was a thing—he just liked wearing them. One time, he tried busking on the sidewalk with devil sticks during the middle of a class trip.

But that was Evan. He'd constantly say or do these insanely inappropriate things—maybe despite the fact that they were inappropriate, or maybe because of it. And all the same, he was my friend—again, maybe despite the way he acted, or maybe because of it.

For quite a while there, he and I were as close as could be.

And now, as I keep saying, he's gone.

Evan passed away in the summertime, in the August after I started working on this book. We'd been very close in high school, but at some point during college, we fell out of touch, and somewhere along the line, he got into drugs. Hard.

Looking back, I think every one of us who knew him must have known Evan was dabbling in drugs—more than dabbling, really; at risk of succumbing to them. But none of us ever said anything about it all—to a parent, to him, nobody. Now, a decade and a half later, I'm left here trying to figure out: why didn't we?

Was it just because we were all so focused on finding our way through that transitional time in our lives that we didn't concern ourselves beyond what we could see in the mirror? Or was it because we were flush with hormones, rebelling against rules and just somehow unable to fathom saying anything of substance to a parent, anything that felt like squealing? Maybe it was just that we were afraid to stand out—afraid to say something and be wrong?

We weren't blind and deaf. Everyone, I think, saw or heard something. Hell, most of what we heard came from him! We'd come back from college on a break or whatever, and he would tell us that back on his campus, he had just been robbed at gunpoint by angry pot dealers.

Thinking about it now, it seems impossible to imagine being told something like that and not talking to parents, to police—to him, even, to sit him down and say that whatever he was doing had to stop. But I can still remember that even as he talked about being assaulted over drugs, he laughed. He was laughing! I didn't ever know if I could take him seriously, and maybe that was part of it: Evan was both relentlessly positive and unafraid to lie.

I don't mean that Evan was dishonest, because he wasn't. I mean that Evan liked to tell whoppers like a game—for fun, to see what he could get people to believe. I remember him telling my parents that he was dating a Playboy model, and not when we were little kids, either—when we were seventeen or eighteen! At that age, we were too old for grandiose, childish fibs like that, but he insisted it was true. We all knew it was bull, but Evan didn't care.

So maybe that's why when Evan came out with a story that, as I look back, sounds like a cry for help, we never said anything. Maybe we figured he was just messing with us. Robbed at gunpoint? A kid from our school? Get out of here.

But maybe we should have listened. Maybe we should have paid better notice.

After all, look what happened in the parking lot of our local diner.

•

I can't help but realize that over and over, I've written *we*—but really, I mean *me*. I can't speak for anyone else. I can only speak for myself. *I* waved off any notion that my friend might be in trouble. *I* didn't say anything.

A number of our social studies teachers mentioned Kitty Genovese while we were in high school. She's famous in New York—other places too, probably. Back in the '60s, living in New York City, Kitty Genovese was attacked twice by the same assailant in two separate incidents that took place on the same night. She was raped outside an apartment building and left in the street, and almost an hour later, her attacker came back to the same place to find her bruised and beaten body and murder her. Her death is famous, because in that crucial hour between the two assaults, no one stepped in to help. All the witnesses, and there were many in the apartments surrounding the scene, either misconstrued the situation or thought someone else would do something. Every individual ignored the problem. No one came to her aid until it was too late.

So there's precedent for me not reaching out to my friend, I guess.

That doesn't really make it better.

•

As I said, Evan and I fell out of touch during college, and I didn't hear from him—or really even much think of him, if I'm honest—for the next half-decade. But at some point between then and now, Evan and I reconnected. Not personally, just digitally: we became Facebook friends, though "friends," as an English professor, is a word I despise in this context for its acute lack of meaning. I proclaim "Words mean things!" to my students all the time; I scribble the phrase in the margins of their papers as I implore them to edit their work and find the right word to convey their intent—but as well I know, "friends," outside the ecospace of Facebook, doesn't mean a thing. Evan searched my name or I searched his; one of us clicked a button, and the other clicked back. That was it. That was our refurbished "friendship."

When we reconnected, he was in Minnesota, I think. I saw that on his page, and at the time, my mind immediately went to the word "rehab." I didn't know if that was indeed the case, but Minnesota made me think right away of the Mayo Clinic. Looking at his presence online, I remembered what he'd seemingly bragged to me long ago, and saw the slogan for himself he'd typed onto his profile page: "There is a God. I'm living proof."

I surmised that maybe he had done some deeply harmful—self-harmful—things in the years. But whatever that entailed, he seemed to be putting himself back on track.

Eventually, we did talk a little bit—exclusively online. He told me he was indeed in rehab, and that he was completing his degree. This was five years after I had graduated; 'til then, I'd had no idea he hadn't finished.

At the end of our conversation, he gave me his cell number, but told me not to spread it around because he was on the run from the cops.

I blanched.

He admitted that he'd been lying about being on the lam. I didn't call.

After that, I forgot about him, and I got along with my life for a while.

•

Sometime later—six years later, in fact—Evan moved to Los Angeles, the same city where I live. Either I saw a Facebook post of his, or he saw a Facebook post of mine, and we realized that we—once companions on the lowest rung of the high school ladder, fellow members of the quiz bowl and the chess club and countless other socially unattractive activities—were now, about twenty years later, both in the same place.

Evan reached out to me online once more. He asked to hang out and again gave me his cell phone number, telling me he was making LA his home for a while. It reminded me of how close we'd been when we were nerds in high school.

This was 2014. Earlier that very year, my favorite actor, Oscar winner Philip Seymour Hoffman, died of a heroin overdose. In one of his roles I loved best—as Lester Bangs in *Almost Famous*—he said, "The only true currency in this bankrupt world is what you share with someone else when you're uncool."

I thought of that while looking at Evan's glowing message on my Facebook screen. We'd shared an awful lot of that currency as youths.

But a lot had happened since then. And when he extended that invitation to reconnect, I didn't respond.

In fact, I ghosted. I never called him. I never messaged him again.

I'm not proud of it; I have been on the other end of that and I know it's not a good feeling. But when Evan suggested that we meet up, I disappeared.

Why? I think, more than anything, that I was scared. I didn't see Evan anymore as the kid I'd been in all those classes with in high school, or as the guy who forgave and forgot our eighth-grade fistfight to grow into a close, close friend. I saw him as a person with a disease that frightened me—as though, just by being around him, I could catch it.

I'm not proud of it, but it's true. I thought of his addiction and I thought *criminal*, and I pushed our past aside. It didn't matter than I knew he wasn't a bad guy—that he wasn't a monster like Andrew Kehoe, Jenelle Potter, or John Orr. I just didn't want to think about the unpleasant world of addiction and drugs. I pulled the blanket over my head and made sure my ankle wasn't hanging over the side.

Then I forgot about him all over again until I found out that he died.

CHAPTER 8

——

New York City—Louis Eppolito

To everyone he grew up with in East Flatbush, a working-class neighborhood in Brooklyn, Louis Eppolito represented a great American success story.

Eppolito was named for his grandfather, a Neapolitan immigrant born Luigi Ippolito who, though he didn't speak a word of English, came to the United States in search of a better life for his family. When the elder Luigi—"Louie the Nablidan," as he came to be known—arrived, he availed himself of just about the only profitable work available to an Italian in New York at the dawn of the 1900s: the mob. Three of his sons—James, Freddy, and Ralph—would later join the mafia as well, finding shelter in the Gambino crime syndicate, and by the time Louis was born to Ralph in 1948, the family was well ensconced in organized crime. But while he watched his father, uncles, and even his cousin turn to a life of crime, Louis went the other route.

At age 21, Louis applied to join the NYPD. He did have to lie to pass his background check, of course, falsely claiming that he bore no relation to any members of organized crime syndicates. The truth did eventually come out, but by then, it was not only too late, it didn't matter: Louis was a good cop.

By the early 1980s, Louis had been promoted to the rank of detective. He'd spent a decade making collars in the roughest neighborhoods of Harlem and Bedford-Stuyvesant, and after that, he was assigned to the NYPD's Organized Crime unit, with a special focus on criminal homicide. It became his job to investigate the very mafiosos who populated his neighborhood—who shared his DNA—and the killings they perpetrated, but that never slowed him down. He continued to receive commendations. He married and had four children, and his oldest daughter used to recall him boasting all the time at how well he'd done on the straight and narrow. "I'm the son of a Gambino crime soldier, but look what I have made of myself!" she recalled him saying.

He was highly decorated. He was well respected. He had even, he was proud to point out, been awarded the Medal of Honor for his work protecting the citizens of New York.

Eppolito had defied his roots. He managed to make a good life, and he was proud of it. All in all, Eppolito's story seemed picture-perfect, but there remained with it just one problem: it wasn't the slightest bit true.

•

On the morning of February 10, 1986, a New York-area jeweler named Israel Greenwald prepared to leave the house to go to work. Before stepping out, he kissed his two daughters goodbye.

They would never see him again.

Greenwald was in his thirties, still young, on the last day of his life. He'd been born in Israel just after World War II, and after relocating briefly to South Africa to apprentice in the diamond business, he moved to America, where he found work as a jeweler.

Greenwald's job involved significant international travel, as well as the handling and transporting of precious stones—and of course, large sums of money. As Greenwald prepared for one of his many business trips to London, a professional contact asked him to cash a bearer-payable US treasury bond for him while abroad.

Though this request may seem unusual now, at the time, such an act was not uncommon—particularly in the Orthodox Jewish community of which Greenwald was a member. As a consequence of WWII, many wealthy Jews had grown to distrust lay financial institutions. Rather, they utilized—and in some cases, continue to utilize to this day—trusted go-betweens, rather than national banks, to handle their large financial transactions.

Greenwald agreed to cash the treasury bill abroad, accepting the standard offer of a small commission for his assistance. Unfortunately, unbeknownst to Greenwald, the treasury bill was stolen. Its receipt was immediately noted by the international law enforcement community, who notified the IRS, and upon returning to the states, Greenwald was intercepted by the FBI.

He was shocked to learn that he'd unwittingly been duped into fencing stolen property. When informed of this, Greenwald agreed to confront his colleague. He was an upright citizen, an upstanding man—and as such, he also agreed to record the conversation.

This decision proved as unlucky for Greenwald as the treasury bill itself. His contact, as it happened, was mobbed up, and had received the note as part of a mafia heist. What's more, when Greenwald did engage him in conversation, the man found Greenwald's FBI recording device.

At that point, Greenwald's days were numbered. He went missing on February 10. A few days later, his car was found, abandoned in the long-term parking lot at John F. Kennedy International Airport. Greenwald himself, however, was not. Had he simply run off? Though it seemed unlikely, it was certainly possible, especially with his car at the airport—possible enough, at any rate, that Greenwald's life insurers refused to pay off on his policy, sending his family, now bereft of their breadwinner, into penury to go with their grief.

It would take nearly two decades before anything conclusive could be said about the fate of Israel Greenwald. His beloved daughters never gave up hope, but they never got any closure, either…until 2005, when his corpse—complete with a matched pair of bullet holes penetrating the back of his skull—was exhumed from under the floor of a Brooklyn auto mechanic's.

•

Louis Eppolito retired from the NYPD in 1989, a twenty-year veteran of the job. Though his record was officially clean when he left, his reputation was shrouded in suspicion. The first report to note his potential corruption was filed in the late 1970s, right around the time his uncle James and his cousin James Jr. were murdered by other members of the organized crime community. It seemed their multi-million dollar charity scam, the International Children's Appeal, brought unwanted attention to the syndicate. They brazenly swindled such visible public figures as Senator Ted Kennedy and First Lady Rosalynn Carter, even getting their photos in the newspaper with these lawmakers, and that brought too much heat to bear. They were executed behind a Coney Island high school at dawn.

After identifying the crime scene, Eppolito was approached by mobster henchmen and asked to accept a payment in condolences for their deaths.

This brush with both death and the law did nothing to temper Eppolito's actions—if anything, it only exacerbated them. By the mid-1980s, Eppolito had been suspended after being charged with getting too close with the criminals he'd been tasked with investigating—specifically, for passing confidential information to high-ranking members of organized crime. He fought the case and beat it in court, earning himself reinstatement; all the same, almost all of his police colleagues began to withdraw from association with him—save one: his partner, Stephen Caracappa.

Eppolito and Caracappa were both NYPD detectives, but there their similarities ended. Eppolito was intimidating and physical; Caracappa was slight and introspective. Eppolito's close associates outside the police department were the mobsters he was raised with; Caracappa's were the FBI agents he worked alongside on a joint task force.

Eppolito knew what the mobsters knew about organized crime and the police. Caracappa knew what they *wanted* to know.

Together, they made a dangerous pair.

•

In 1992, Simon & Schuster published Eppolito's memoir, which he titled *Mafia Cop*. A line from the first chapter—written by Eppolito's co-author—reads as follows:

When we were introduced in the spring of 1990, Detective (Ret.) Louis Eppolito was six months off the job, and the first words out of his mouth were, "You know, I didn't do it."… [W]hen a cop blurts out to a journalist that he "didn't do it," the odds are better than even that he *did*.

"It," as Eppolito referred to the word, meant what he'd been charged with: passing along confidential information to members of organized crime families. Indeed, the district attorney's office felt certain enough of Eppolito's guilt to charge him. And despite the fact that Eppolito was found not guilty, the whole experience, by his own admission, soured him on his career and the police force as a whole.

He made fewer high-profile arrests. He spent more time accepting comped meals and drinks at mob-run establishments.

More and more, he became an enigma, a walking contradiction in terms. He railed against cops he saw as crooked, and at the same time, he constantly bad-mouthed the force. From citizens, he violently demanded adherence to the law, but he saw himself as above it. "If any citizen dared file a complaint with the Department's Civilian Complaint Review Board, [I] did the expedient thing: [I] lied," he wrote in his autobiography. As he described an off-duty raid he organized against a number of homeless drug addicts, he went on:

> We broke their hands. We broke their arms. We broke their legs. And we did it viciously. I had one guy on the ground… and I whaled him, twice across the face with a board. He was barely semiconscious when I sat down on the curb, picked up the biggest rock I could find, and crushed every one of his fingers, one by one. I could feel the bones smash. Then

I went to work on the other hand. Finally, I snapped both his wrists before cracking him over the head with a brick. We put thirty-seven people in the hospital that night, and not one radio car responded. There were ambulances galore, and several of the junkies, including the guy whose hands I mangled, ended up crippled for life. And I didn't give a fuck, and I still don't.... When you work on the street, you abide by the law of the street.

Eppolito's corruption trial took place in 1985. He loudly proclaimed his innocence. The very next year, bodies started to pile up.

•

As Louis Eppolito wound down his career on the police force, he began to turn his energies to two other fields: writing and acting. He craved notoriety, riches, and fame, and for Eppolito, the world of entertainment seemed a likely font for all of the above. His first pursuit, writing, led to the aforementioned publication of his memoirs; in them, he portrayed himself as a vigilante, happy to dance along the cliff face of legality as he both flouted the law and openly consorted with made men from his old neighborhood.

His second pursuit, acting, allowed him to do more or less the same.

At the tail end of his cop career, Eppolito scored a cameo in the movie *Goodfellas*—weighing north of 230 pounds, he played a character introduced by Ray Liotta as "Fat Andy." This bit part led to him meeting actor Joe Pesci; they later bumped into each other in a New York cafe, and Pesci helped Eppolito land roles in such other movies as *Predator 2, Ruby, Bullets Over Broadway,* and *Lost Highway.*

In all these films, Eppolito played one of two types of roles, exclusively: a cop, or a mafioso.

It may have been make-believe, but it was hardly a stretch.

> At the times pertinent to the Indictment, the New York City Mafia consisted of five organized crime families: the Bonanno, the Colombo, the Gambino, the Genovese, and the Lucchese. The government's key witness at trial was Burton Kaplan, a former associate of the Lucchese Crime Family who had been involved in, inter alia, narcotics trafficking, sales of stolen goods and misbranded clothing, and attempts to negotiate stolen financial instruments...
>
> In the early 1980s, Kaplan had been in prison with Frank ("Frankie") Santoro, Jr., who was loosely associated with the Gambino Crime Family. In late 1985 or early 1986, after both men had been released from prison, Santoro approached Kaplan and said that Santoro had a cousin who was a police detective, who...would, in exchange for money, provide Kaplan with law enforcement information **and other types of assistance.**
>
> —*US Court of Appeals, Second Circuit, Docket Nos. 06-3280 / 06–3396;2008.*

What other types of assistance exactly were being sought out at that time by Burton Kaplan and his *caporegime,* Lucchese underboss Anthony Casso, would not come out for years—not until long since people had started to disappear.

The first to go was Israel Greenwald. When Casso heard about how Kaplan's T-bill heist had gone south and how the fence had agreed to cooperate with investigators, Greenwald, he decided, had to be dealt with.

Come February 1986, he got his wish.

Under the guise of a traffic stop, two cops Casso knew pulled Greenwald over and told him he was wanted in connection with a hit-and-run. They removed Greenwald from his car and put him into their unmarked cruiser—but they never brought him to any stationhouse for questioning. Instead, they took him to a friendly auto body shop, where the only questions asked were answered by the reports of a service revolver.

The next person on Casso's list was James Hydell, a young mob associate who had recently botched an attempted on Casso's life. Hydell, much like Greenwald, was pulled off the street and told he was wanted for questioning, but he, too, never saw a formal booking. Instead, he was stuffed inside a trunk and beaten to a pulp outside a Toys R' Us on Flatbush Avenue.

He was murdered later that day.

The third person Casso had offed with the help of his cop hitmen was a man with the almost comically stereotypical name of Nicky Guido. Casso's undercover agents pulled his address off an NYPD computer, and on December 25, 1986, gunned Nicky down outside his house while showing his dad his new car.

As it happened, that killing proved to be problematic, because as it turned out, Nicky Guido was not a mobster.

There *was* a mobster named Nicky Guido. However, that's not the one who got killed. The Nicky Guido killed on Christmas Day, 1986 was a phone company employee who'd just started the process of joining the New York Fire Department. Nicky Guido the mafioso lived a few miles away in another part of Brooklyn, and when he heard about the Terminator-style attack on his namesake, he fled the state.

The police officer hitmen cooled it down for a while after that.

•

Louis Eppolito retired from the police force with a pension in late 1989. He moved to Las Vegas and kept appearing in bit parts in films as he began to pen his own movie scripts, many based loosely on his life. His taste for self-promotion—piqued by years of feeding arrest reports to the press—he kept up as well, even going so far as to appear on *Sally Jesse Raphael* to promote the release of his book, *Mafia Cop*.

During that episode, he spent half an hour detailing for all of America just how good a cop he'd been despite the background he'd had to leave behind. And among all those Americans watching the program was Betty Hydell, a woman who recognized the retired cop on TV as the very man who'd taken her son in for "questioning" all those years ago—just before he disappeared forever.

She bought the book. She flipped to the clutch of photos in the middle. And then, she recognized the second cop who'd pulled her son James off the street that day: Stephen Caracappa, Eppolito's partner.

It took time to build up a body of evidence, but eventually, Eppolito was arrested once more, and his second trial was far different from his first. He wasn't charged with corruption, but with racketeering and murder. The racketeering was difficult, as it involved a statute of limitations, but after Eppolito convinced his own son to provide meth and ecstasy to undercover agents—agents that he thought were film financiers interested in his stories—he was finally brought in.

His partner, who'd since moved to Las Vegas to join him in retirement, went down too. They couldn't have known that they were targets. They couldn't have known that Burton Kaplan and Anthony Casso, their old undercover bosses, had been arrested, flipped, and turned state's evidence against them. And they couldn't have known that investigators had been able to dig up poor Israel Greenwald's body.

At trial, Louis Eppolito and Stephen Caracappa were found guilty of eight murders, all executed for hire for the mob. Their favorite tactic—using an unmarked police car to pull over victims—came to light, as did just how little it cost to buy his gun and badge: $4,000 a month, with a bonus bump for murders.

All in all, Eppolito and his partner earned just under $375,000 from the mob. When the crooked cops came to justice, their actions would end up costing the state of New York $18.4 million in restitution.

At last, Louis Eppolito, who had spent years proclaiming how much he hated cops who'd been bought off, was unmasked. Curiously enough, it was in no small part his failure to learn from his uncle's mistake—to stay out of the limelight, to eschew his thirst for fame—that became his undoing.

As a postscript, one man killed thanks to Eppolito was never mentioned at trial: Bruno Facciolo, a mobster murdered by his own after Eppolito exposed him as an NYPD informant. In truth, Facciolo had never been a collaborator, but he *was* the man who had killed Tommy DeSimone—the real-life inspiration for Joe Pesci's character in *Goodfellas*.

CHAPTER 9

—

Manchester, NJ—Joseph S. Portash

"Look at the garbage board." Follow the trash. That's all Thomas Peele had to go on.

It's all the anonymous caller would tell him.

Peele got the call on a late fall afternoon as he sat at his desk in Toms River, a small, central New Jersey suburb of about seventy thousand people. It was 1988, and broad political and social conservatism had recently become the new norm. People were afraid of the inner cities, crack was sweeping the nation, and violent crime was on its way to an all-time high. More and more, the affluent were rushing to the suburbs, fleeing to the relative safety—and then-record low property tax rates—of suburbia.

Peele had recently moved down from New York, and he was trying to make a name for himself as a gritty, old-style investigative journalist. His beat was a suburb a few miles away: Manchester Township. About half the size of Toms River, it was home at the time to just about thirty thousand people—almost all of whom, directly or indirectly, were there thanks to the efforts of Joe Portash.

Portash had all but built the town, developing it out of his own vision and dedication. When it came to the health and viability of Manchester, Portash had much to take credit for.

And, as Peele would soon discover, credit wasn't all Portash had been taking.

•

After the close of World War II, America grew at a previously unimaginable pace and in a theretofore unseen way. Whereas people had for generations turned away from rural lives to migrate to the city, postwar Americans, benefitting from rising income, increased demands for space and luxury, and the widespread availability of cars, drove the creation of suburbs and exurbs, commuter towns that allowed for access to population centers while offering greater freedoms and fresh air. Throughout the 1950s, areas all around major cities like Boston, Chicago, New York, and Philadelphia saw suburban havens blossom and grow.

Despite this nationwide boom, as late as 1960, Manchester Township, New Jersey remained home to fewer than four thousand people. Hard to believe, given its auspicious location: an hour and a half from New York City; an hour from Philadelphia; less than that, even, to the state capital of Trenton; and just thirty minutes from either the tourist-friendly boardwalk at Seaside Heights or the bustling army base at Fort Dix. And yet, it remained small.

At this time, Joe Portash was a land planner for Ocean County, a civil service job he'd earned after returning from service in the Korean War. However, Portash saw the opportunity for more— both for himself and for the sandy, pine-addled land in the center of the area he oversaw. The region was near government, city life, and leisure; it was also relatively flat and, therefore, would be relatively straightforward to develop. A population that had hovered around one thousand from the Civil War through World War II had effectively doubled in each of the two decades since, meaning that though it still wasn't large by any stretch, there was obviously enough demand to sustain a growing town.

But how could he make Manchester stand out? Surely, there were plenty of other parts of the country that could accommodate the growing hunger for homeownership—indeed, many other areas already had. The solution he reached was ingenious: planned seniors communities.

Senior living, in the form of nursing homes or retirement homes, was a well-established idea by 1960. Planned communities were, as well: William Levitt, the father of modern suburbia, had already launched his third eponymously-named suburban development in as many states by then—the third such town, in fact, sat in bordering Burlington County, and its population had swelled in the past ten years from under nine hundred to over ten thousand! But combining the two was an innovation, and to Portash's mind, it was key to growing Manchester: *planned seniors communities!* As residents, senior citizens were ideal: they had money, providing a solid tax base for public funding and development, and what's more, they required few municipal services: less crime meant less spending on police; fewer children meant less spending on schools.

With Portash planning, Manchester at last found its chance to grow, and grow it did. But Portash was not content to sit on the sidelines and watch. He wanted to get into the game. In short order, Portash abandoned his bureaucratic position with the Department of Planning and established himself in two elected roles: one as a member of the Board of Freeholders, the standing legislature of Ocean County, and the other as the mayor of Manchester Township.

At around this time, the Manchester town government established a relatively new municipal charter structure. It called for a mayor, supported by and selected from a five-member Township Council, who would control the governance of the burgh in tandem with the elected body.

It was supposed to bring about transparency, mutual responsibility, and separation of powers. What it actually brought was cronyism. Because when Portash supported a candidate, who would deny him, the man who brought life to the town from nothing? And when he called upon those elected officials who owed their jobs to him to carry his water, how could they say no?

Portash first took the Manchester mayor's office in 1962. He'd hold the position, whether in name or *ex officio*, for a stunning fourteen year stretch. During that time, Manchester's population more than quadrupled, as more and more developments with names like Leisure Knoll and Crestwood Manor sprung from the loam. And as Portash's impact swelled—to say nothing of his godfatherly relationship with the residents who made up the voting populace— he only further consolidated his power.

Portash sat on both sides of the scales local government. There were no checks and balances; he controlled the mayoralty and the Council, too, to say nothing of the zoning board and the departments of water and power, and by the end of the 1960s, any contractor hoping to so much as dig a hole for a new home in Manchester couldn't get in without Portash's say-so.

One such contractor was a man named Robert Schmertz.

•

Robert Schmertz was a New Jerseyite born and bred. He grew up in Hackensack, and by his thirties, he'd become a successful real estate developer based in Lakewood. He launched his planned senior living communities—newly built single-family residences designed for and sold to those already in their golden years—in Lakewood as well, and when he began seeking to expand, he looked right down the road to Manchester Township.

And to Joseph Portash.

Portash welcomed Schmertz's revolutionary idea of creating housing developments specifically for retirees—indeed, it played specifically to Portash's aims for Manchester. By the mid-'60s, however, Portash had not only secured his position at the seat of local power, he had grown all too happy to abuse it.

Schmertz, Portash decided, was going to be allowed to develop his senior living communities in Manchester—but for a price. It wasn't until after Schmertz greased the wheels with a $30,000 bribe, disguised as payments for fictional "consulting" work that Portash never performed, that construction on Schmertz's senior housing developments could begin.

Schmertz's money bought him favor with Portash, which by extension got him in with the town legislature, too. His company won zoning approvals not only for valuable development deals, but also for free access to city-owned sewer and water lines. Constructing and maintaining those access lines should have put millions of dollars directly into the city's coffers—but it didn't. Portash directed his cronies whom he'd helped onto the Council to ensure that Schmertz's payola brought him free access to those services as well.

Of course, Portash didn't stop at basic fraud. He also proved to be a skillful master of graft. In one of the more impressive financial swindles of Portash's time in office, the Manchester Council approved a land swap that led to the city trading away its claims to valuable central real estate in exchange for another plot that was almost worthless. In fact, the land Manchester Township government gave away almost immediately sold for a price over *one hundred times* the appraised value of the land Township had received in trade.

None of Manchester's citizens were aware of this at the time, of course. It didn't come out until far, far too late.

•

In early 1975, Robert Schmertz was indicted for bribing Portash. The case was so damaging that the multi-millionaire Schmertz was forced to sell off his interest in the N.B.A. champion Boston Celtics, lest the league seize control of the team entirely. Interestingly, though Portash himself was the public official at the heart of Schmertz's bribery case, he was neither tried nor named as a co-defendant.

Why not? Because Portash was the one who ratted out Schmertz.

In exchange for becoming a prosecution witness, Portash received full immunity for all the felonious behavior to which he readily admitted at the grand jury hearing—which was a lot. Curiously, the case never even went to trial—after the grand jury voted to indict, Schmertz suffered a stroke and died. Portash was later tried on separate charges, but due to the immunity he'd been granted, he was unable to take the stand in his own defense, and the US Supreme

Court ruled he could not be fairly tried despite the numerous acts of gross criminality he'd committed while sitting as mayor.

As disgusting as all this behavior was, this run-of-the-mill corruption was, sad to say, none too unfamiliar in politics of the time—and especially not in the great state of New Jersey. (Just three years later, another New Jersey mayor and a New Jersey senator, as well as multiple congressmen and other civil servants, would begin taking bribes to sell Atlantic City casino rights and illegal immigration papers to foreign nationals, as fictionalized in the Oscar-winning film *American Hustle*.) However, what made Portash's swindling of the public particularly odious was his behavior in the years *after* he admitted taking bribes.

·

"Look at the garbage board." Thirteen years later, that's all the frightened voice on the phone was willing to tell Thomas Peele when word got around that Peele was still looking at Portash, trying to figure out how much influence he still wielded—and how crooked Portash still was.

"It's a sham," the caller told him. Then he hung up. But it was enough to convince Peele to continue to dig.

Portash stepped down from the mayoralty after he was indicted for and admitted to corruption. For many, this would signal the end of a reign—but not for Portash. Even out of office, he still controlled local politics, and when it came time to replace him, only one candidate ran for the position: his own wife.

Adie Portash took over the office of mayor of Manchester Township in 1975, and for years, Portash continued to control the town through her. A few years later—the very week after Portash's conviction was overturned by the Supreme Court, in fact—Mrs. Portash came to decide that Manchester Township needed a business manager to help keep its affairs in order. She created the position, attaching to it a $65,000 salary—equivalent in today's dollars to roughly $250,000 per year—and went directly to the one man she had in mind for the windfall job.

Her husband.

Floating down from his court case on a civic-funded golden parachute, Portash's thirst for wealth and control never slaked for a moment. As it happened, there were other people in Manchester who found themselves growing quite thirsty as well: the residents of Manchester's largest development, Pine Lake Park.

Pine Lake Park was one of the first communities built in the early days of Joe Portash's regime. Unlike some other projects, it was built without connection to citywide piping systems, instead relying on a local underground aquifer for its water. As mayor, it was Portash's job to ensure that the local military bases—to say nothing of the enormous chemicals plant just a few miles down the road—did nothing to sully that groundwater source.

It was not a job he took to heart.

By the 1980s, Pine Lake residents had begun to fall seriously ill. Mothers suffered astounding numbers of miscarriages and stillbirths. Teenagers came down with diseases that usually struck septuagenarians. Eventually, the town had to bring in fire trucks to provide safe water to residents one hand-carried jug at a time. But by then, the public had been awakened to the problems, and people started to demand answers.

Portash did his best to silence his critics the one way he knew how: money. He and the then-mayor—one of the beneficiaries of Portash's political patronage—paid off the leaders of the water protests, giving them jobs with the city to hush up. This silenced them for a time, but other voices rose to fill the vacuum. One such outcry came from Art Silverstein, a retiree, the very kind of person Portash had sought to bring to the town in the first place. But Art Silverstein was not just any old retiree: he was a retired accountant, and he couldn't help but notice that property taxes in Manchester seemed to be growing at an astounding rate. In fact, by his calculations, Manchester had come to levy one of the highest levels of taxation in the nation. There were still relatively few public services called for in Manchester… so where was all that money going?

Working together, Silverstein and Peele sniffed out the jobs handed to the former Pine Lake protesters, and they got to the bottom of the anonymous caller's garbage board fiasco, too. It seemed Portash's mayor was paying himself a few extra thousand dollars a year to sit on a sham municipal waste disposal board that accomplished next to nothing and hardly, if ever, met. His appointment to that board had never gone through a political approvals process, either: Portash had simply mandated it one day, and the next, it happened. That's why the taxes had gotten so high: the public money was being diverted to political quid-pro-quos—and lord only knew what else.

This public unmasking of the town's deep-seated cronyism finally awakened its residents, and on Election Day in 1989, they took to the polls. Demanding reform, Manchester Township elected to move to a standalone mayoralty separated from the powers of an independent Town Council. They also voted in attorney Jane Cordo Cameron to the Mayor's office, pushing out the string of Portash's longstanding lieutenants.

As soon as the vote passed, Portash fled the state, decamping for Maine before the new nonpartisan government could take effect on July 1, 1990. He didn't want to be there when the truth came out, it seemed. Because when the members of the new government did take over, they found that Joseph Portash had done far worse than support favored colleagues or businessmen during his time at the helm of Manchester. He'd single-handedly looted the entire town treasury.

•

Three months after the shift in Manchester's government, the *Philadelphia Inquirer* chronicled the gross malfeasance unearthed during Portash's reign, filing this piece about the last of his handpicked successors, Ralph Rizzolo:

> On Rizzolo's last business day in office, the last Friday in June, police officers at their headquarters next door to the town hall noticed that municipal employees were carrying boxes of files to Township trucks.
>
> Following in unmarked cars, the officers saw the workers dump the records at the county landfill and watched Rizzolo direct them, pointing where he wanted the papers dropped, right where sewage sludge would be sprayed on them.
>
> When the workers left, police confiscated the records and called the County Prosecutor's Office.

When [Jane] Cameron took office July 1, she said she found $2.80 in the Township legal fund and $240 in an engineering fund. "We didn't have any money," she said. "They cleaned out everything."

A subsequent, thorough accounting showed that Portash had the town keep two sets of books, stringing along the public the whole time with phony ledgers as he stole countless millions of dollars. Most of that money he blew in Atlantic City, but some he siphoned off to pay for his second home in Maine or other real estate investments. He got so brazen that he sometimes didn't even bother to cover his tracks, occasionally simply writing out checks directly to himself or to other members of the Council.

Unfortunately, Portash for a second time escaped prosecution for his crimes. While in exile in Maine in February 1990, Portash died of a massive cardiac arrest, possibly caused by the stress of waiting for all the damning evidence against him to come to light. While Portash again avoided the courts, however, his puppet cabal did not: a number of the members of Portash's Township Council ended up in jail for corruption.

The city, meanwhile, was left all but insolvent after his reign. As for the chemicals plant that was poisoning Pine Lake Park, it became a Superfund site. With polluted water and no money to speak of, Manchester Township was forced to build anew at the dawn of the '90s—this time, following someone else's vision.

Luckily for residents, it was a far sight clearer.

CHAPTER 10

—

Kerrville, TX—Genene Jones

It happened almost faster than young Petti McClellan could understand. Her daughter Chelsea, not yet two years old, had been fine just that morning. She'd only come in for a routine checkup—and yet, within minutes of arriving at the pediatrician's office, Chelsea turned blue, and she stopped breathing. Dr. Holland and her nursing staff swarmed to action, trying desperately to resuscitate Chelsea and snatch her back from the jaws of death, but they failed. In the ambulance rushing from the clinic to the hospital, Chelsea McClellan's heart stopped.

In the frantic rush that followed, no one so much as glanced at Petti—if they had, they would have found her with her palm pressed against her face. She was alone, inconsolable, watching from the sidelines, unable to comprehend or accept that that her formerly healthy, happy infant had just died before her eyes. As the nurse carried away her baby's remains on that otherwise fine, sunny Texas morning, Petti began to wonder: what could have possibly gone so wrong, so quickly?

·

When pediatrician Dr. Kathleen Holland opened her Kerrville clinic in September 1982, she was all too happy to welcome Genene Jones to the staff. Jones came to tiny Kerrville, population 15,000, by way of San Antonio, one of the largest cities in America, and she brought with her four years of work experience and a stunning recommendation from the pediatric ICU at Bexar County Medical Center, the largest hospital in the region. Holland herself had earned her medical degree not far away, at the University of Texas in Austin, and she was excited to count such a seasoned local hand as a member of her staff as she launched her private practice.

Kathleen Holland trusted Genene Jones, so much so that Holland not only gave her a nametag reading "Pediatric Clinician"—an overly lofty title, but one that she hoped reflected the esteem in which she held the nurse—but also opened her very home to the woman. Dr. Holland sublet Genene Jones a room in her house, inviting Jones to live with her, her two kids, and their babysitter as Jones acclimated to the new position.

Holland didn't know that she'd just opened her doors to a killer.

•

Genene Jones had, by all accounts, a sad and affecting childhood. Immediately after she was born, she was abandoned by her parents. She grew up in an adoptive family of six, and she was often forced to fight for attention in that large home. When she was a teenager, one of her foster brothers accidentally blew himself up while messing around with homemade explosives. Soon after, both her other foster brother and foster father followed along to the grave, each succumbing to cancer. Her foster mother, grief-stricken, began to drink.

In the aftermath, Genene Jones became lonely and traumatized, and she also became overweight—not an easy set of circumstances in which to develop. Immediately after finishing high school, she fled from her pain, though hardly into better circumstances: just weeks after her graduation, she married a high school dropout named James DeLany.

Their marriage was hardly pacific. It does not serve him well to note that, after failing to earn his own degree, DeLany spent his time trying to pick up schoolgirls. Within months, DeLany informed Jones of his plans to enlist in the Navy. Jones responded by claiming she was pregnant. DeLany grudgingly stayed, but when Jones's claim in short order proved itself to be false, he enlisted, packed up his things, and moved to Georgia.

Jones followed her husband, and in time she did conceive, but as so often happens when a marriage is already on the rocks, the child failed to save their union. The pair broke up, and even as Jones became pregnant with a second child, they divorced. Suits and countersuits followed, and it all ended up with Jones returning to, of all places, the very home that she had fled: her foster mother's house. She brought with her two little kids, no education beyond high school, and nothing much at all to do.

·

Genene Jones had always loved children and had always wanted to have kids of her own. Strange, then, that when she split from her husband and moved back to Texas, she almost immediately deposited her children with her foster mother—but though she may have been a drunk, she at least offered childcare gratis, and Jones used that free time to undertake a year of vocational instruction in nursing at a San Antonio public technical education center. There, she earned her certificate and passed her licensing exam, and soon she began to look for work as an LVN: a licensed vocational nurse.

Despite having no college experience, Genene Jones had little problem finding a job. San Antonio was booming at the tail end of the twentieth century, growing by over ten percent each decade, and Jones was hired at Methodist Hospital before even completing her licensing requirements. It seemed an auspicious vote of confidence in her and her skills—curious, then, that she was asked to resign eight months later. So began a trend.

From Methodist, Genene Jones moved to South Texas Medical Center; at that hospital, she lasted only three months before moving on. Despite a resume studded with these poor performances—positions marked by clashes with other staff members and by surprisingly frequent trips to the hospital of her own—Genene Jones managed to find herself at Bexar County Medical Center, the newest hire into the pediatric intensive care unit, in late 1978. It was there that she'd come meet Dr. Kathleen Holland, a country doctor who in short order became impressed by Nurse Jones's seemingly endless desire to learn, provide input, and be present for the delivery of care to her patients.

It was also there that infant bodies started curiously piling up.

•

Chelsea McClellan was born on June 6, 1981. Sensing she'd finally been given the little angel she'd always hoped for, her mother, Petti, had her tubes tied. While Chelsea had been born slightly premature—she'd spent just eight months in utero, rather than nine—and she suffered spurts of troubled breathing on occasion, she was, for the most part, a healthy baby girl. Petti, for her part, was a diligent mother, taking her daughter regularly for care at the newest, most modern pediatric clinic in Kerrville: the practice of Dr. Kathleen Holland, staffed by LVN Genene Jones.

On Friday September 17, 1982, McClellan brought her daughter in for two inoculations. Dr. Holland ordered Nurse Jones to prepare the shots.

Genene filled the syringes in another room, out of sight of anyone else, but that didn't raise any eyebrows. Both Dr. Holland and Petti McClellan trusted Jones completely. Why, when little Chelsea had suffered a spell of loss of breath during an earlier visit, it had been Jones who alerted the doctor, Jones who placed the oxygen mask over the tiny baby's mouth, and Jones who carried the baby into the back of the ambulance and sat with her as they rushed young Chelsea to nearby Sid Peterson Hospital. Jones, McClellan believed, had saved Chelsea's life that day—who better to trust?

However, when Genene Jones gave Chelsea the first of her inoculations on Friday, September 17, something odd happened. The girl's breathing slowed. McClellan told Jones to stop, but Jones insisted on giving her the second shot. That's when the one-year-old turned blue, ceased breathing, and began having a seizure.

That day, young Chelsea McClellan died—a nightmare for any mother. But though she was soon laid to rest, the nightmare was far from over.

•

At outset, no one knew what really happened to Chelsea McClellan. Healthcare professionals initially chalked up her untimely demise to Sudden Infant Death Syndrome, or SIDS, a catchall term used to describe otherwise unclear cases in which very young children simply die during development. However, as it became clear to members of the South Texas medical community, something else was going on.

The ER staff at Sid Peterson Hospital noted that Chelsea's was only the most recent in a spate of major patient emergencies—all disproportionately stemming from what should have been a quiet, small-town pediatrics office. Dr. Holland had been in private practice for only a month and worked in a town of just 15,000 people, yet somehow, her young patients seemed to be a constant presence in the Sid Peterson Hospital emergency room:

- On August 24, Chelsea McClellan was first admitted with seizures and respiratory arrest.
- On August 27, Brandy Lee Benites was admitted with seizures and respiratory arrest.
- On August 30, Chris Parker was admitted to the ER with breathing trouble. On that same day, Genene Jones began to treat another boy in the ER, Jimmy Pearson, despite the fact that he wasn't even her patient. Immediately after she injected the boy with an unknown drug through his IV line, over other emergency medical personnel's objections, his breathing stopped and his heart failed. He died.
- On September 3, Misty Reichenau was admitted with seizures and respiratory arrest.
- On September 17, Chelsea McClellan again had seizures and respiratory arrest. This time, she died.

- Also on September 17—that same afternoon—Jacob Evans was admitted to the ER, apparently also due to seizures and respiratory arrest.
- On September 23, Rolinda Ruff was admitted to the ER with respiratory arrest.

One after another, these seemingly healthy children were rushed out of Dr. Holland's clinic and into the ER, all suffering from sudden loss of breathing—and all coming directly from Genene Jones's care. There was, it seemed, a pattern in the data. Time and time again, infants were falling into states of critically compromised health. There was also a slate of eyewitnesses to these emergencies, some of whom began to realize that something just wasn't right.

Consistently, Genene Jones was noted to exhibit odd behavior during these traumatic episodes. Over and over, Jones demanded of paramedics, registered nurses, and even doctors that she be the one to oversee patient care—unusual behavior for a vocational nurse with just one year of medical schooling. She also seemed to relish these crises, reaching what was described as an almost blissful state in the emergency room, feeding off the energy of trying to pull patients from the brink of death to the point where colleagues thought she appeared borderline orgasmic.

On September 23, the day Rolinda Ruff was rushed from Dr. Holland's office to the Sid Peterson Hospital emergency room fighting off respiratory arrest—the seventh such youth in a month—anesthesiologist Frank Bradley happened to be on call. He attended to young Rolinda along with a number of other doctors, and he watched as the infant struggled to move her arms and fight against the tube that had been inserted into her throat to help her breathe. Almost immediately, he recognized her movements: they were the very same he'd seen in the operating room as patients awoke from doses of succinylcholine.

As the Bexar County Medical Examiner Dr. Vincent Di Maio would later explain while reviewing the case, succinylcholine "is a synthetic paralytic drug often used to relax clenched throat muscles when inserting emergency breathing tubes. It takes effect within seconds but lasts only a few minutes, long enough to intubate a struggling patient."

In other words, it's an anesthetic, and it is normally used only by three types of medical professionals: ER doctors attempting assisted respiration, anesthesiologists preparing for surgery...and executioners delivering convicted murderers a lethal injection. In large amounts, succinylcholine does more than relax the throat muscles: it causes the lungs to stop functioning altogether. It very quickly leads to death by asphyxiation, and for that reason, it is often the second of three drugs administered by the state in killer cocktails to the condemned.

F. Lee Bailey, the famous trial attorney who successfully defended O. J. Simpson, once called succinylcholine the perfect murder weapon, because the drug is quickly broken down by the body, and it vanishes with hardly a trace. Very few people can recognize the symptoms of an overdose...few, thats is, save anesthesiological experts like Dr. Frank Bradley, to whom it was immediately clear that this little girl had been injected with it.

In short order—the next day, in fact, after Dr. Bradley witnessed the struggles of Rolinda Ruff—the senior staff of Sid Peterson Hospital stripped Dr. Kathleen Holland of her admitting privileges. Bradley went a step further, telling Dr. Holland that if she herself hadn't administered succinylcholine to patients, she ought to take a good, hard look at her nurse.

•

When Genene Jones left Methodist Hospital in the winter of '78–'79, her first job out of vocational school, it was reportedly due to conflicts with a doctor over patient care. She said that doctors didn't want to give the best care to patients; coworkers, however, said that she tried to boss the doctors around and tell them what drugs the patients needed. She lasted just eight months at Methodist, which seems like quite a stretch compared to the paltry three months she made it through at her next job at South Texas Medical Center. Jones quit that that position, electing to undergo a minor surgical procedure at the medical center and not return to work. These behaviors—demanding more and more attention, and more intense care for patients and for herself—were not isolated.

Genene Jones, it became clear, displayed pronounced symptoms of Munchausen syndrome, a psychological condition in which people feign or exaggerate illnesses and their severity in order to garner comfort, attention, and feelings of strength and control. She also displayed the symptoms of Munchausen syndrome by proxy, inflating her patients' complaints and illnesses in order to secure more care and more focus for them—and more adulation for her when these over-inflated problems were solved.

In some instances, these attention-seeking behaviors led to praise from doctors and other nurses, but in others, it led to conflicts, as Jones became bossy and demanding when coworkers and supervisors refused to accede to her wishes. What's more, over time, even these exaggerations of needs unfortunately ceased to be enough, so Jones was forced to synthesize a surer way to draw attention to her adeptness with critically ill patients: to actively make her patients become critically ill.

When Frank Bradley, the anesthesiologist, shared his suspicions regarding succinylcholine with Dr. Holland, she informed him that her clinic had never administered any of the drug. However, when she returned to her offices, she began to develop doubts. There had been an instance in which the clinic's lone bottle had been brought out during a patient episode, then disappeared. Genene Jones, in fact, had been the one to inform Dr. Holland that the bottle had gone missing, and it had been Jones who had marked it as such in inventory and ordered another supply.

Within days of Dr. Bradley giving voice to his misgivings, Jones approached Holland and told her that—miracle of miracles—the missing bottle of succinylcholine had been found. Holland examined it for herself, however, and she found that the safety cap was missing from the top of the bottle. What's more, there appeared to be two large needle holes in the stopper.

"How do we explain this?" Holland asked. Tellingly, Jones replied to Dr. Holland—her boss, her housemate and her friend—"I think we should just throw [the bottle] out.

"We thought the bottle was lost," Jones would say, her voice steely and calm. "We should say we never found it."

Dr. Holland blanched. Was Jones really suggesting that they intentionally cover up facts tied to the death of one of her patients? She began to agree that Dr. Bradley was onto something—something almost too horrible to name.

•

That same afternoon, Petti McClellan visited the grave of her daughter, as she had nearly every day since the child had been interred. On that day, however, Petti was confronted in the cemetery by an unexpected sight. When she reached her daughter's tombstone, she found another person already there: it was Genene Jones. The nurse was on her knees, rocking and crying in a near-catatonic state and calling Chelsea's name over and over. Petti McClellan reached out to Jones—and the moment Genene noticed another person was there, she gathered herself and quickly scurried away.

Jones returned to Dr. Holland's office, sedate but far from calm. She was distraught, she said. She also informed Holland that she needed medical care, as she had just intentionally overdosed on prescription pills.

Holland dutifully called an ambulance, which rushed Jones to the emergency room. There, it was discovered that she had taken only four pills, hardly enough to be concerned about, let alone to have her stomach pumped for. It was just another flare-up of Munchausen syndrome, Jones's need to be coddled and focused upon. But as Jones spent time resting in the hospital, Holland continued to pursue her misgivings about the nurse. She shared her findings regarding the succinylcholine bottle's mysterious disappearance and signs of tampering with another doctor, despite Jones's remonstrations, and she also had the contents of the bottle analyzed. It turned out that though the bottle appeared full, lab tests showed it contained only about fifteen percent of the drug by volume—the rest had been replaced with saltwater, as if someone, like a kid trying to hide having stolen nips from a parent's liquor cabinet, was attempting to cover his—or her—tracks.

Over the following days, more lab tests were performed—and not just on the bottle, either. Earlier that year, a team of European researchers had published a paper in the *Journal of Analytical Toxicology* explaining their groundbreaking new methodology for doing what had previously not been thought possible: finding concentrations of succinylcholine in embalmed human tissue.

County investigators ordered the body of little Chelsea McClellan exhumed. Her tissue was analyzed, and the results were conclusive: without a doubt, succinylcholine had been present in the little girl's body when her lungs seized and she died.

That was enough for both the medical community and law enforcement. Dr. Kathleen Holland summarily fired Genene Jones. Shortly thereafter, Genene Jones was indicted for murder.

•

Jones was charged with only one murder, that of young Chelsea McClellan. However, as investigators dug deeper into her past, it became quite clear that children seemed to die around Genene Jones all the time. In fact, some *twenty* babies had died under Genene Jones's care in the pediatrics ICU at Bexar County Medical Center during an eight month stretch alone. But when Jones took a month-long leave of absence—to check into the hospital herself, undergoing another minor (and perhaps unnecessary) surgical procedure—there wasn't a single unexpected death in the pediatrics ICU.

Joyce Riley, who worked as a Patient Care Systems Analyst in Bexar County Medical Center, noticed this statistical aberration.

Her job was to review records and data to try to piece together information about recordkeeping standards and quality of care in the hospital. Generally, she worked in other areas of the hospital, but when a colleague took vacation leave, Riley began to investigate the data at the pediatrics ICU and found what to her seemed to be incontrovertible statistical evidence that something foul was afoot. As she would later state:

> I had heard in the past a number of rumors that there were babies dying on the 3 to 11 shift.... I began to look at who was taking care of those babies. And it happened to be one of the unit's finest nurses: Genene Jones.
>
> ...[The director of the unit] truly thought Genene Jones was the outstanding bedside nurse in the unit. But by 1981, we'd all learned that it seemed like Genene was increasingly at the center of problems and controversy in that unit...
>
> [A young patient] slipped into cardiac arrest. Genene Jones was assigned to him on the evening shift. She was the first one to arrive to do CPR. [A doctor] who was covering pediatrics that night took over the [emergency] code when he arrived. He assisted the child, injected two rounds of cardiac drugs, then used a defibrillator, but the baby didn't respond. Genene Jones began to suggest medications to the doctor as an LVN. The doctor ignored her. She repeated herself, her voice got angry, and [the doctor] said, "Shut up!" to Genene Jones. He snapped at her. He was trying to concentrate on what he was doing, because he had a dying baby on his hands. Then Genene started saying, "You need to give certain drugs; you need to give certain drugs!" He refused to acknowledge her

existence, and Genene started to hyperventilate. She collapsed into a full asthmatic attack…

They declared [that patient] dead. Four years later, the investigator on this case said, "That is, we believe, the first of the murders that Genene Jones committed." The reason Genene Jones was yelling, "Give this drug, give this drug, give this drug!" is she knew what she had given that child to create the [emergency] code. This is what we found out later: Genene knew why the codes occurred; she knew the antidote drugs. And she passed out in an asthmatic attack because she knew the doctor was not going to give the [right] drugs to save the baby, and she knew the baby was going to die.

Riley was certain she had identified Jones as the culprit, and there could no question about the data: among nearly all the life-or-death emergencies in the unit, Jones was the common factor. Indeed, Jones's 3-to-11 p.m. shift began to be known among nurses in the Bexar County Medical Center pediatrics intensive care unit as the Death Shift. However, when Riley brought this information to hospital administrators, they buried it. Afraid, ostensibly, that the hospital would be sued if the information ever came to light, they instead promoted and transferred Riley to a position that kept her away from all patient data, and they dismissed all the unit's Licensed Vocational Nurses—including Genene Jones.

They claimed it was because they wanted to require all working nurses to have a higher standard of education, to have earned their registered nurse's licensure, and that it had nothing to do with anyone's individual performance. In fact, despite the misgivings of the nurses and doctors who'd worked with her, Bexar County Medical Center even gave Genene Jones a glowing recommendation as they showed her the door—which made it all too easy for her to land a new job, with fresh access to more defenseless babies just like Chelsea McClellan.

•

The trial was a media circus, not least due to the fact that Jones kept on talking to the press, despite the recommendations of her attorneys. The trial was also relatively short. Genene Jones was found guilty of murdering Chelsea McClellan, and she was sentenced to ninety-nine years imprisonment. In a separate trial, Jones was handed a concurrent sentence of sixty years for injecting another infant named Rolando Santos with what should have been a lethal dose of the blood-thinning drug heparin. Though the baby survived, "he just bled from every orifice in his body," said the district attorney.

With 159 years of jail time ahead of her, it certainly seemed that Jones would die in prison. Unfortunately, these court cases would not mark the end of this manipulative murderer's story.

•

Jones's two sentences were concurrent rather than consecutive, meaning that she could serve each at the same time. Additionally, a prison reform law designed to ease overcrowding made it possible for convicts to receive as much as triple credit for time served— meaning they could be locked up for as little as one third of their sentence and still complete their jail time.

Despite intense outcry from the Kerrville and San Antonio communities, including former victims and their parents (as well as the now-grown Rolando Santos), Genene Jones's conviction became one of these scheduled for early termination of incarceration term. The date of her scheduled release from prison—not parole, but outright release—was set for early 2018.

At the time of her imprisonment, Jones was suspected of killing as many as forty-six babies. However, she was only charged with and convicted of one murder. One of the major reasons for that was Bexar County Medical Center's apparent fear of wrongful death civil suits—the very malfeasance that abetted Jones's continued practice of deathly medicine.

In the early 1980s, while the district attorney was in the process of determining whether or not to prosecute Jones on additional counts, Bexar County Medical Center shredded its pharmaceutical records for the years when Jones was an employee there, stopping only when the DA's office received a tip from an informant that the document destruction was taking place. A *New York Times* article reported that the "Dean of the University of Texas Medical School at San Antonio, which uses the Bexar County Medical Center as a teaching facility, was [also] cited for contempt of court for failure to turn over full and complete records of an in-house inquiry into the deaths."

The D.A.'s office estimated that four and a half tons of potentially relevant files were destroyed. Because the paper trail detailing Jones's actions during these sprees was lost, there appeared to be insufficient evidence to charge her for any of the murders she committed before moving to Kerrville.

•

In the years since Genene Jones murdered Chelsea McClellan, the crime that finally brought her serial attacks to light and put her behind bars, Petti McClellan became a nurse herself—not an LVN as Jones was, but an RN, a registered nurse, the kind who could have kept her job in Bexar County's pediatric intensive care unit even after the hospital's self-serving purge.

On September 17, 2016, Petti McClellan posted a message to her own Facebook wall, lamenting all that had taken place and all that could have—and should have—been done. She wrote:

> Today I sit here thinking about my daughter Chelsea McClellan. I wonder what she would be doing in life, would she have a family, even what she would look like. These are things I will never know. I will never know because thirty-two years ago today Genene Jones made the cold blooded decision to murder her. She did this without any regard to her precious life! She did this without any regret. She did this to protect herself from being found out what she had been doing to infants for years! How many she murdered in San Antonio will anyone ever know for sure? I doubt it. While no one made any effort to protect the babies in San Antonio, not the doctors, nurses (any who tried were fired), not the administration of the hospital. She was allowed to go to Kerrville per request of Dr. Holland to be her nurse at her new clinic. Therefore she was allowed to begin killing again! And that she did! Which is how Chelsea became her first victim in Kerrville…
>
> My heart breaks I still cry when I think about what could have been. So she will walk and once again no one will be there to protect the children. My advice for anyone that has

children to keep tabs on where she ends up because I know this Psychopath and she will kill again!

Love and Miss You Chelsea.

However, unbeknownst to Petti McClellan, Jones did *not* walk. In the summer of 2017—mere months before she was set to be released, and decades since she'd seen the world outside of a prison cell—Genene Jones was charged with two other infanticides: killing eleven-month-old Joshua Sawyer in December 1981 with injections of an anti-seizure drug, and killing two-year-old Rosemary Vega in September of the same year with an injection of an substance unknown.

As of early 2018, Jones had been indicted by a Bexar County grand jury in a total of five new murder cases, all dating back to the early 1980s. Her release date remains unknown, but one thing is certain: she will, thankfully, remain in custody for quite some time to come.

CHAPTER 11

—

Chillicothe, MO—Ray & Faye Copeland

Most people don't stay long in Chillicothe, Missouri. Even people born in Chillicothe tend to head out in search of something more. Despite a healthy birth rate, the area has hardly grown at all for the past hundred years, and the reason is straightforward enough: save farmers and the few businesses that serve them, there's not all that much going on. However, in the mid-1980s, a string of men arrived in Chillicothe and found they just couldn't leave.

By the '80s, there were only two types of farms still solvent in Chillicothe and the little burghs in Livingston County, Missouri, that surrounded it: very large farms and very small ones. The financial crises of the mid-1970s killed off the midsize plots, local growers who borrowed big and swelled quickly, only to fall prey to rising rates of variable interest and plummeting prices of commodities. Big-time agri-business with big-time financial backing was happy to snap up all of that land, and come the end of the decade, the only farmers left standing were either so large as to be able to cruise over the economic storms, or so small that they had been able to wait out the squalls unharmed.

The Copelands fell into the latter camp.

Ray and Faye Copeland owned a forty-acre plot about ten minutes west of Chillicothe proper. Though they'd had six kids, none of their children stayed to work the land after they'd grown. As Ray and Faye aged, this came to pose a problem: how could a seventy-something farmer and his sixty-something wife keep on making their living off that little plot of earth?

In time, they hit upon an answer—and it was one that would inscribe them both into the annals of infamy.

•

In small farm towns, just about everyone meets at the diner, feed store, or cattle auction to discuss weather, local politics, and crop yields. Ray, however, never took part. He was dour; he grunted only the fewest words possible to answer direct questions or get what he needed, and he was never once known to smile. Still, no one thought he was a bad man. After all, how bad could a person be in the farmlands of Chillicothe?

Unbeknownst to the Copelands' neighbors, the answer was: very.

Despite looking the part of the wholesome if ornery small-town farmer—right down to the denim overalls he wore every day—Ray Copeland was anything but. Though his neighbors didn't know it, before moving to the relative quiet of the Missouri pastures, Ray Copeland had spent decades in and out of jail.

In his heart, Ray Copeland was a scam artist. He came about it honestly, to be sure. Copeland grew up in the Ozarks of the Dust Bowl era, when there was precious little work to be had and even less food to eat. He was raised to believe that wits were a crucial ingredient to survival, so his reliance on those wits—as well as his attempts to outwit everyone, from the government to banks to even family members—became a defining characteristic of his existence.

Unfortunately for both him and his wits, Ray just wasn't that smart, and time and again, his efforts to beat the system got him in trouble. For his misconduct as a boy—stealing hogs from his father and selling them; stealing Depression-era WPA checks from the mailboxes of brothers and neighbors, forging their signatures and cashing them—Ray caught whippings. As a man, though, Ray's crimes sent him to jail—repeatedly. His rap sheet was long as a Midwest summer's day, and it read like the mid-century equivalent of a streetwise gangbanger's:

- Stealing horses
- Stealing cattle
- Forging personal checks
- Forging government checks
- Knowingly passing bad checks

In between stints in jail, Ray met Faye Della Wilson, and he convinced her to marry him. This had no effect on his behavior, however. As Ray grew older, he and his wife kept moving ever northward, trying to stay a step ahead of the law. It didn't work. Indeed, he kept getting caught, eventually earning the dishonor of being imprisoned in just about every state along the Mississippi River. Once, he even had to serve his time breaking horses on the sentencing judge's farm. The last of Ray's escapades took place in Bloomington, Illinois, and at that point, Faye put her foot down. They were trying to raise a family, and Faye was sick of watching Ray get hauled off to jail. He'd have to leave his criminal past behind him, she told him—or at the very least, quit getting caught.

Copeland said that he understood—and with that, he picked up stakes and moved the family to tiny Chillicothe.

•

One nice thing about Chillicothe was that there just wasn't any crime—not crime as we think of it, anyhow. Sure, people got into bar fights come a Saturday night here or there, but there was not really theft or serious violence to speak of. After all, the only people living around Chillicothe were a band of small farmers, all of whom knew one another. Frankly, it didn't seem as though anyone had anything worth stealing.

It was in this environment that the Copelands bought a farm and raised their brood. For a time, all was quiet, if not exactly happy. Once those children aged, though, and Ray and Faye were left to run the plot alone, they found themselves in trouble. After all, they could hardly scrape much of a living off the land. They needed another a way to make money, and after some thought, Ray figured he hit on one: cattle. He might be too aged to raise much in the way of crops, but he could, he was certain, buy small herds of cattle and resell them at a markup. There was only one problem: he didn't have any capital.

To get started, Ray swallowed his pride, walked into a bank, and took out a small loan. He attended a farm auction, where he bought a couple head of cattle and resold them. It wasn't enough, though, and Ray found himself unable to pay back the money he'd borrowed. Growing up through the Great Depression as he had, Ray already hated and mistrusted bankers and banks, and it didn't take much to turn him. His neighbors didn't know it, but angry and broke, Ray decided that it would be much easier to make money selling cattle if he only didn't have to pay for the cattle to begin with.

The next time Ray went to a farm auction, he bid on his cattle like before, but when he won, he just bounced a check. It would be days before anyone would discover his account was overdrawn, and in the interim, Ray resold the cows for cash and buried the proceeds on his farm in a jar. When the bank came calling about the bad check, he just turned out his pockets and shrugged his shoulders—leaving the local auction house to have to swallow the loss.

Word traveled quickly about Ray's struggles, like word does in a small-town. Despite this, fellow Chillicotheans still didn't think Copeland a bad man, just another fellow farmer having trouble in tough times. Of course, after a few more winning bids went unpaid, the farm auctions stopped selling to Ray altogether, which got Ray thinking: even if the auctions wouldn't sell to him anymore, they would surely still sell to *not* him.

Ray began driving eight hours round trip back to the last place he'd called home before Chillicothe: Bloomington, Illinois. There, he started picking up out-of-work drifters staying at the YMCA. He offered them a day's work and a good day's pay to, as he told them, help him buy cattle.

Once they agreed, Ray would drive the men to auctions. They'd sit apart from one another, but the men would watch Ray for agreed-upon signals and bid for him by proxy. When the men won, Ray would give them one of his checks, which they'd sign.

Ray would resell the cattle that same day, then drive his hiree back to Bloomington, never to see one another again. When the bank withdrew money, Ray would protest: sure, it was his account, but the signatures on the checks weren't even his. He'd be right, of course, and once again Ray managed live his dream of selling off cows he'd never had to pay for.

Up to this point, people still didn't think too ill of Ray Copeland. Sure, he kited checks. He'd been doing so all of his life, just like Dick Hickock of *In Cold Blood*. In that place and time, it wasn't even all that uncommon. But it wasn't check scams that brought the sheriff down on the Copelands. No, what sent Ray—and his wife—up the river for good was when men started going down from Bloomington to Chillicothe and then never coming back.

•

It all started with a phone call: a man who once worked on the Copelands' farm informing an anonymous tip line that he'd been scared for his very life. Ray Copeland had pointed a rifle at him, he said. He'd only barely escaped, he said. And while working on the farm, he said, he'd seen bones—and not cattle bones, either.

Human remains.

The police weren't convinced, but they searched the Copeland homestead anyway, and while what they found wasn't exactly incriminating, it was indeed curious: a guest bedroom stuffed to the gills with piles of mismatched men's clothes. The clothes came in all shapes and sizes, none of which were Ray's. They spilled forth from the closet and under the bed. Some bore nametags—again, none of which were Ray's—and the names didn't even all match.

Faye had an explanation: they were from farmhands, she said, people who'd worked there but left, leaving their shoddy rags behind. It would have been plausible enough, but for the sheer volume of clothing, enough to almost fill a whole room. If they were just forgotten clothes, the police wanted to know, why on earth were there so many?

A further search turned up a list. There were names on that list, all names of men who'd worked on the Copeland farm—and alongside those names, there were notes. The list read, in part:

>Gary Misko—left
>the Big Fat Man—back
>Jim Harvey—X
>Jim Geer—back
>Wayne Freeman—X
>Jack Holiday—back
>Robert Root—back
>Thomas Park—X
>Paul Cowart—X

The men marked "left" had moved along down the road. The men marked "back" had been returned to Bloomington. But the men marked with an "X"?

After working on the Copeland farm, no one had never heard from those men again.

Not long after, the Prosecuting Attorney for Livingston County, Missouri, would present this list at trial. He knew, he said, what had happened to those men marked on the list with an "X": Ray Copeland had killed them, dropping each one with a .22 rifle round delivered to the back of the head.

What's more, Ray Copeland was illiterate, meaning the list wasn't even his own—it had been drawn up by Faye.

The townspeople were aghast. On its face, the claim seemed outlandish, almost impossible. How could a septuagenarian kill all these able-bodied young men? And even if he could do it, physically, from a psychological standpoint, why on earth would he? What motive could he have had?

Furthermore, how could anyone believe that Ray's wife, Faye—sixty-something and mother of six—would take part in such a spree too, serving as the secretary to death?

All in all, it was a tough notion to fathom, and it might well have been an impossible story to believe—that is, of course, were it not for all the bodies.

•

In the fall of 1986, Ray Copeland picked up Dennis Murphy in Bloomington, Illinois, with the promises of three hots, a cot, and fifty dollars a day for helping Copeland in purchasing cattle. Murphy agreed, and on the ride to Chillicothe, Copeland explained to Dennis Murphy the role he would play.

Copeland was getting old, he said, and losing his hearing, which made it hard for him to keep up with what auctioneers were saying in their hyper-fast prattle. It would be Murphy's job to go with Copeland to farm auctions to bid on and purchase heads of steer.

It was the same scam Copeland had run years prior, but in the time since he'd tarnished his good name with his neighbors, Copeland had added a few extra wrinkles. The first step was to take Murphy to a post office in nearby Ludlow, Missouri, to get him a PO Box. Next, Copeland gave Murphy a wad of cash to open a checking account at Citizens Bank and Trust, using Murphy's PO

Box as his address of record. The checks would be sent to Murphy's PO Box and be drawn in Murphy's name now—not Copeland's.

When the checkbook arrived at the post office a few days later, Copeland took Murphy to a livestock auction. While still a few blocks away from the venue, Copeland pulled over and asked Murphy to get out of the car.

"It's because people don't like me," Copeland told Murphy. "If people know we're working together, they'll overbid just to spite me."

Murphy told Copeland he understood and agreed to walk the rest of the way. Once inside, Murphy watched for Copeland's hand signals and bid as Copeland instructed him to, buying thirteen cattle for $2,784 and paying for it with a check of his own. Of course, there wasn't that kind of money in his checking account, but Copeland told him not to worry about it—he'd deposit the cash into the account later that week to cover the purchase.

That same day, Copeland resold the cattle and pocketed the cash. Twice more that week, Copeland took Murphy to livestock auctions and had the man walk in on his own; Murphy bought a dozen head of cattle for $4,116 at the first of those shows and twenty-three head for $6,832 at the next. In both instances, Murphy wrote the checks himself and Copeland immediately resold the cows, quickly netting cash worth almost $50,000 in today's money.

As they drove off from the last of these sales, Copeland asked Murphy to write him a check as well—a blank one. "So if we should both die in a wreck or something," Copeland said, his wife Faye could clean out the checking account.

Murphy did as he was asked. And with that, his useful life to Ray Copeland was over.

•

Over the next few years, a number of drifters came through Chillicothe, passing bad paper at a slate of farm auctions before disappearing into the mist. At first, law enforcement officers suspected that perhaps Ray might be up to his old check-kiting tricks, but when they asked him about the men, he had an alibi. "Dennis Murphy? Sure, I know him. I hired him on for a while. Hell, he got me, too," he'd say, and then dig up the very check that Murphy had signed over to him on their last day together. "If you find him, give *me* a call."

After that, the investigations died down—officials chalked it up to drifters running quick scams and moving on; nearly impossible to trap and catch—and from then on, Ray Copeland enjoyed free rein to mastermind bouncing checks again.

For years that followed, Copeland drove back and forth to Bloomington. Time and again, he hired tramps like clockwork, and he never saw an ounce of trouble pulling off his con—until, that is, he picked up Jack McCormick.

McCormick was in his fifties, older than most of the men whom Copeland had worked with—older, craftier, and wiser to the ways of the world. Jack McCormick seemed to sense right from the jump that Copeland was doing something unsavory with his checks and his cattle auctions—hell, McCormick himself had been known to sweet-talk his way into driving a car right off a salesman's lot now and again—but for a while, he allowed himself to go along for the ride. Still, McCormick kept an eye open at all times. The disheveled pile of mismatched clothes spilling out of every corner of the bedroom assigned to him gave him pause, just as it had to the cops many years prior. Copeland's insistence that McCormick neither bring anyone over nor tell any family or friends where he was staying troubled him, too. In short order, there would be even more to set off McCormick's alarms.

A few weeks after McCormick arrived on the farm, Ray Copeland knocked on his door with a .22 rifle in hand and asked for his help in removing a rodent from his barn. There was a raccoon that had crawled in behind some hay bales, Copeland said; he wanted McCormick to take a stick and poke around to scare the critter out. "You flush him out, and I'll shoot him," Copeland told McCormick—innocuous enough, but something just didn't feel right. The whole time, McCormick did his best to stay close to old Ray. He took care not to fully turn his back on the old man either, and for the one brief instant he did glance away, when he looked around again he could have sworn that Copeland was pointing the rifle almost right at him.

That did it. On the spot, Jack McCormick quit, and he insisted Ray Copeland drive him into town. When Copeland took McCormick to the bank to close out his checking account and refund the money Ray had made him deposit, McCormick escaped. He ducked out a back door, found himself a car, and then got himself far the hell away from Chillicothe.

Once he'd safely made his way across the state line, he picked up a payphone and made a call.

•

Sheriff's deputies and townspeople alike were skeptical from square one. Old Ray Copeland a murderer? It just didn't add up. Of course, that didn't stop the local media from swarming in once word leaked what was being posited, and soon, there was a firestorm…just little to feed it. Investigators had found the clothes and the list, and that presented enough probable cause to keep them looking, but there didn't seem to be much else. They expanded their hunt to neighboring farms where they knew Copeland had worked handyman jobs, but for days, nothing turned up. It all seemed a crank, a coincidence, and the lawmen were on the cusp of calling everything off…until, in a barn a few miles from the Copeland homestead, deputies found a spot where the hard earth had been tilled soft.

They grabbed a trowel. They began to dig. And soon enough, they turned up an old shoe—with a foot still inside it.

That foot led to a leg, which led to a body. "Boys," said Livingston County Sheriff Leland O'Dell, "watch those damn reporters down the road, and keep this off the radio for a while.

"Better keep looking," he continued. "May be more in here."

Indeed, there were more: three corpses in total, all sharing a long ditch of a grave. A fourth body was found on the farm soon thereafter, hidden under a massive load of a hay bales. Later, a fifth would be dredged up from a well on the property, a concrete block and a rope lashed around the dead man's pant leg and the name "Dennis"—as in Dennis Murphy—shining from his belt buckle.

Each of the dead boasted .22 rifle holes in the back of their skulls. As it turned out, they'd all also last been seen alive around the time they'd started working for the Copelands.

•

The response in the small—and formerly quiet—town of Chillicothe was instant. Shocked citizens swarmed the courthouse, eager to better understand what on earth had been transpiring right under their noses. "You listen close for me tomorrow morning," exhorted one retiree to her friend on her way out of the courthouse one evening. "I've got a doctor's appointment."

Ray Copeland was found guilty of five counts of murder—not surprising, given the clothes, the bodies, the testimony placing him with the men in Bloomington and at auctions, the slew of checks, the checklist, and of course, the rifle. Ray tried to plead guilty in exchange for a life sentence, but in a rare turn, the judge rejected the plea and forced a trial. At that trial, Copeland received the death penalty—making him, at age seventy-six, the oldest man in the USA to ever be sentenced to death.

Copeland's wife Faye was also tried. In a separate trial, she, too was convicted for the crimes. "I never done nuthin!" she reportedly cried, and while it may be true that she never fired any of the fatal shots, prosecutors argued and the jury agreed that Faye was complicit throughout. She fed the men while they lived in her home; she abetted Ray's scheme to lure, lull, and murder. And of course, she kept all the records—the records of employees hired, and the records of the men killed.

Ray Copeland showed as little emotional concern for his wife of more than fifty years—even as she was presented with a guilty verdict of five counts of premeditated murder—as he ever had to the neighbors he'd disdained at the local diner. When he was informed of her sentence—death by lethal injection, which incidentally made

Faye a perfect complement to Ray as the oldest woman in America on death row—Copeland simply replied, "Well, those things happen to some, you know."

In the end, both the Copelands did skirt the executioner's chair: Ray was struck down by Father Time before the needle could get him, and due to her own failing health, Faye's sentence was commuted and she lived out her days in a convalescent home. All the same, Ray and Faye Copeland unquestionably left their indelible mark on Chillicothe, Missouri, forever. Sindy Thomas, a captain in the Livingston County Sheriff's Office, which is based in Chillicothe, who began her career right around the time of the Copeland investigations, spoke to as much.

"It was shocking.... I mean, for something like that to happen in a very small community, especially where we live? Because they were people that were your neighbors, you knew 'em...

"They are still, to this day, talked about. It is still a part of our community."

At the very least, the livestock auctions nowadays no longer accept unsecured checks.

CHAPTER 12

—

Evan (Continued)

I'm still not done talking about Evan.

Like I said, I learned about Evan's death from my Facebook feed. Following his page—feeling suddenly much more interested in and connected to him now that he'd passed and it was no longer possible to actually meet face-to-face—I saw that he'd overdosed.

A part of me felt justified in not having reconnected with him: he wasn't a hard drug addict, recovered. He was a hard drug *user*. He'd been leading that double life. That part of me, with a concurrent voice trumpeting loudly in my mind, told me that I'd made the right decision in icing him out. Online, I found out that the same year he'd tried to reach out to me, he had been charged with narcotics possession not once but twice: once before he moved to LA, and once after he'd already arrived.

In other words, once before he contacted me, and once after.

So there it is, that part of me thought: I had done the right thing. It wasn't only that associating with drug users would impact what others perceived about my character; if he was out there possessing drugs, that meant he was buying them too, and who knows with whom *he'd* been associating and what *they* might have done to *me*: a guy who works in a school program hand-in-hand with police, helping guide youth who would like to join the ranks of law enforcement. Forgetting for a moment the stain reconnecting with him could have left on my professional credibility, the very people he knew could have been dangerous to me, and that meant he, too, was dangerous. *Quod erat demonstrandum.*

That was one part of me, and true, I couldn't dispute the argument it presented. But the rest of me—and it was a much larger part—still felt terrible.

Whatever else had been the case, Evan needed help. That much was clear—that much, I had guessed at well before he even told me. He was an addict, yes, but he'd tried to quit: I knew as much from the countless posts I read on his Facebook page from his friends who (unlike me) had been close to him 'til the end, who knew what he'd gone through and knew that he indeed had gone to rehab over and over and tried, desperately, to kick substance abuse. On his own page, he'd described his job title as a Sober Companion—despite his own problems, he was trying to do what I could not: offer help to those who needed it.

•

After his passing, Evan's family arranged a memorial for him. They flew out to Los Angeles in the middle of a hot summer to honor his memory on the beach. The part of me that had been feeling so low for not reaching out a hand or doing anything at all save shrink away in fear told me that this was my chance to change—that I should go, that I had to go.

But I didn't. Evan's parents, who'd forgiven and accepted me way back when, and Evan's sister, whom I'd also been friends with back in high school, came out to Los Angeles to host a memorial service to honor Evan's life, and still, I didn't show up.

For a long time, I couldn't come to terms with what I'd done, or even why. Why didn't I go? There was no manifestation of my dead friend's drug addiction that could have harmed me, and I should have shown respect for his passing and our former friendship. Still, I didn't—why not? The more I thought about it honestly, the more I came to realize that it had something to do with fear. Even that, though, was an incomplete answer. Fear or what? What could I have been afraid of?

Was I afraid of sharing in the grief with his family? Was I afraid of the reminder of my own mortality? Was I afraid of being somehow professionally tainted by an association with a now-deceased, unfortunate former drug addict who had been a close friend, when I'd known him, and as a kid had been weird like me?

Honestly, it was all of those things and more.

•

When I was a kid, I wasn't scared of dying. I remember this quite well. Somehow, any death scenario I conjured up in my mind also included me watching my own funeral and hearing people speak well of me, and ended with me miraculously returning afterwards and living all the more confidently for the words friends shared that they thought I'd never hear. (I'd not even read *Huck Finn* by this point—I came up with the notion entirely on my own, and when I did in tenth grade finally read that book and got to Huck's funeral scene, I was shocked to find that Mark Twain had already detailed on paper some hundred years earlier more or less exactly what I'd envisionned.)

If not death, what did scare me as a kid was crime—specifically, the thought of being arrested for a crime I didn't commit. This terrified me. For years during my childhood, I was chilled by the fear of being booked under a case of mistaken identity, or of being framed, and summarily winding up in jail. To me, the threat was as real as the frightening possibility of being forced to eat tuna fish.

Setting aside for a minute the absurdity of an eight-year-old losing sleep over the thought of being set up for a felony, recalling this helped me understand that even as an adult, crime still shocks me. (As it does, I imagine, most readers of this book.) I'm very logical; it just doesn't make sense to me that, knowing the consequences, anyone would choose to commit a crime—any more than, knowing the consequences, anyone would choose to indulge in addictive drugs.

Therefore—and I am certainly not alone in this—on some level, I equate drug abuse to crime.

Make no mistake: drug dealers are criminals; drug trafficking is a crime. But drug addiction? That is not a criminal act. Drug dealers deserve a jail cell, we most all agree, but drug addicts—and again, almost everyone would agree—need help, especially if they're trying in good faith to right themselves and get away from dependency. Of course, countless criminological studies have shown that drug addicts are far, far more likely to commit ancillary, often dangerous crimes against people and property than other members of the general public—of that, there is no question. So maybe it did make sense to dissolve my relationship with a former friend while he was in throes of addiction, even if my support might have helped him. After all, we have all benefitted from the ingrained evolutionary response to fear danger. It is in our nature to avoid situations, places, and people that we believe could cause us harm, and yes, heroin (and those addicted to it) could be dangerous.

But why, then, did I skip out on his *memorial service?* No matter how dangerous the drug (or even the addict) may have been, I couldn't have been hurt, on any level, by joining others in mourning his passing.

·

The more I thought about it, the more puzzled I became. It wasn't just the addiction, I came to realize—it had been the drug. After all, I had known people who had been addicted to cocaine and were in recovery, and I'd known people who'd been addicted to alcohol, and were in recovery—I even knew people who'd been addicted to methamphetamines and were in recovery, and none of those people scared me. I might not have spent time with them or been close to them during their periods of active use, and I was glad for that, but upon recovery, I also never shunned these addicts from my life. I welcomed them back.

So what was it about heroin?

Yes, heroin can kill—but so can alcohol, cocaine, and meth; people OD and die on those all the time, and I didn't lock out everyone I knew who'd ever abused, and eventually quit, those substances. It was something about the fact that my friend had become a *heroin* addict, I realized, that made me shy so far away from him even when he was trying, desperately, to pull his life back together. It was something about that drug that made me, in some part of my mind, lump him in with Jenelle Potter and Carl Gugasian.

Consciously, I knew that he was a danger to himself far more than a danger to me, but unconsciously, some part of me classified him along with dangerous sociopathy. And it had to do with heroin.

Once I realized that, I knew that I had some more research to do.

•

While working on this book, I heard Rose Rudd, a health scientist for the Centers for Disease Control, offer the following statistics in a radio interview.

"When you look at the number of people dying from drug-overdose deaths," Rudd said, "it now exceeds the number of people dying in car crashes...In 1999, there were about eight thousand people in the US that died from a drug overdose involving an opioid. In 2015, there were over thirty-three thousand."

Accidental and unintentional injury is the number one premature killer in the United States. For those under forty-five, drug overdoses have indeed replaced car crashes as the number one source of those injuries, and the number one most lethal drug? It's heroin.

My life experience bears those statistics out. One guy in my grade died from a car crash. Two died from heroin.

There are about 330,000,000 people in America. If 33,000 are dying every year from overdoses of opioids like heroin, that means one in every 10,000 Americans annually is going to die of an opioid OD.

Thinking again of Evan, I headed back over to Facebook. I have about 2,500 friends on there. (Despite my antipathy for the "Facebook friend" term, I do cull people I don't know pretty regularly.) 2,500 friends, and one in every 10,000 Americans dying every year of an opioid OD? That means about every time I get to vote for President, someone I know well is going to overdose and die.

I realized that I'm going to have to acclimate myself to the new normal: learning someone is dead of an overdose is going to be a pretty regular event.

•

Time and again, when I spoke to law enforcement officials while doing research—even those working the small towns forever impacted by the criminals profiled herein—they told me that violent crime wasn't the principal factor tugging their communities apart. It was drugs.

"We don't have many murders here," said Joe Woodward, Chief Deputy of the Johnson County Sheriff's Department in Mountain City, Tennessee, and the investigator on the Jenelle Potter case.

"We have a *methamphetamine* issue here," he said. "And also pills, a lot of pills. Oxycodone. Oxycontin. Morphine."

Captain Sindy Thomas, who began her career under Sheriff Leland O'Dell in Chillicothe, a town nearly a thousand miles away Mountain City, said much the same thing.

"The majority of our crime right now is drug related," she said. "I've seen three generations of family members come through the [criminal justice] system, with all three generations of family addicted to opiates."

The biggest headlines, it seemed—Local Boy Makes Bad!—were reserved for the diabolical folks who lived double lives of crime,

crime that hurt other people. But for each one of those, many more lived a double life of another kind: the kind where the criminals made themselves their own victims.

•

As with John Orr and the rest of the people profiled in this book, I spent time reaching out to people who have known addicts—to people who have been close to and personally affected by *this* type of people leading double lives. Though out of respect, I didn't include their names and their stories, as with everyone else, I found that there were countless people—neighbors, relatives, friends—willing to share their recollections and reflections, if only someone would ask.

In due time, it dawned on me that while I've never come face-to-face with a murderer (I don't think), nor have I ever met a con man (a clever salesman or a smooth-talking beggar, sure, but a *professional* scam artist, never), I have met a fair number of people leading *this* kind of double life. What's more, I'm not alone. Based on the statistics, just about everyone reading this book is probably in the same boat with me.

I wish I had known.

I'm not saying I would have handled receiving the news of my friends' addictions and deaths better—and I certainly don't intend to redirect the focus of this book squarely toward drug use or opioid addiction. I don't aim to politicize or discuss the legal theories of criminality and punishment surrounding those issues, either. As I noted at outset, there are plenty of people out there who know far more about the topic than I do.

It's just that, in the midst of writing a book about double lives in America, I came to realize that *this* double lifestyle is unbelievably common.

Frankly, I wish I had realized this earlier. It might not have made me go reach out to Evan before it was too late—even though having a network of clean and sober people appears to be the best way to keep an addict from relapsing—but it would at least have given me the understanding to find a place from which I could have gone to the beach and given Evan a proper goodbye.

CHAPTER 13

—

Ft. Myers, FL—Kevin Foster

Late on a balmy Florida night in April 1996, four teenage boys sat in a parked car along the side of a quiet residential street. Three of them were archetypal good kids: excellent GPAs, honors classes, superlative winners in their high school yearbooks. They were seniors just weeks away from graduation, and the world spread out before them full of opportunity. They could do anything. They could go anywhere. They could be anyone.

But they couldn't see that. All they could see was the fourth kid in their car: the charismatic dropout. The biggest guy, the most confident. The plan-maker. The persuader. The idea king.

And the one with his hands curled around a twelve-gauge shotgun.

•

If Norman Rockwell had hoped to paint a picture of an idyllic mid-'90s suburban high school, he might well have crafted Riverdale High. With about 1,600 students, the school was a pretty typical top-performing institution: AP classes, an International Baccalaureate program, and an outpost of the Junior ROTC.

Of course, with any school that size, there are going to be cliques: the cool kids, the stoners, the toughs, the jocks. The outcasts. Chris Black was one of those outcasts—he was short, overweight, and more successful in classes than in social settings. He got along with his parents, and his interests hewed to a narrow swath of computing, Dungeons & Dragons, and anime. He was, in effect, a textbook archetype of an invisible high school nobody. Negative three points for charisma.

His best friend, Pete Magnotti, was an outcast as well. Pete was well-known in the school—he was voted "Most Artistic" by the senior class student body, and he had the clear desire to build a career as an animator. However, Pete was short for his age, and he knew it, writing in his diary, "If you're a person of small stature like me, it helps to have big friends."

Pete and Chris had two big friends. One was Derek Shields, an equally scholastically advanced classmate who played in the school marching band and had dreams of working for NASA. The other was Kevin Foster.

While attending Riverdale High School, Kevin had been in advanced math and computer design classes, and he'd showed promise in both of them. But unlike the other boys, Kevin had problems. Real problems. He'd moved around over and over throughout his life, never finding a stable place to call home. His mother, similarly, had bounced from relationship to relationship, leaving Kevin with a revolving door of men he'd call "Dad" throughout his formative years without a single one serving as a lasting father figure.

Lacking much in the way of challenge or discipline, Kevin found himself bored by school, and after his sophomore year, he quit going altogether. His mother didn't mind; in fact, she seemed to like having him around. She owned a pawn shop, and when she came home each day—often with a choice hocked item for her son; in short order, firearms became his favorite—it was nice to have someone to see. Eventually, Kevin began to help her run the store, then was named a co-owner, acting even as a teenager as more an equal to his mother Ruby than a child. In time, Ruby Foster allowed her home to become a clubhouse of sorts, not just for Kevin but for his friends as well.

•

They all had cars. It was a truth about Southwest Florida: you needed a car to get anywhere. Not that there were many places for them to go. Fort Myers offered little for them. They were too young for bars, and Pete and Chris were too small for teen clubs—the kinds of places where bigger boys smoked and jostled for the attentions of girls, shoving young social misfits aside. So they hung around principally with one another, eventually deciding to form a club for themselves—a place where they could be the in-crowd for once, where they could belong.

Basing themselves in Kevin's house, they called themselves the "Lords of Chaos," a name that dripped with overwrought, adolescent bombast—all the more so for their gang symbol: (Ø), a logo that stemmed from an in-joke in their old ninth-grade honors algebra class. After all, how bad could a gang of kids be that chose as their mark a riff on mathematics notation?

Huddled around Kevin's computer, they wrote a manifesto, declaring the formation of the Lords of Chaos and declaring "a campaign against the world. Be prepared for destruction of Biblical proportions," the manifesto read. "The games have just begun, and terror shall ensue."

Then they sent the screed to local newspapers…and went off to bed.

All in all, it seemed to be harmless teen idiocy—at least at first. In time, though, the boys grew bored with just sitting around. They decided they ought to make a little mischief. And that's when things began to spiral out of control.

•

The reign of terror that the boys had promised didn't quite materialize as quickly as the young Lords of Chaos had promised. After all, the teenagers had other concerns to contend with: 10 p.m. curfews, for some, and for others, the jobs working the counter at the local Hardee's, to say nothing of homework. But in time, Kevin's ceaseless influence changed the others. The boys started letting that schoolwork slide, and they began skipping class and putting in hours at the pawn shop instead. It didn't take long for Kevin to convince the other boys to take the next step.

Corralling Chris and Pete into his car, Kevin drove around the Gulf Coast and goaded the one-time honors students into ever more violent and antisocial acts. They started with opening fire hydrants to let loose miniature deluges of water—innocent stuff. Kid stuff. When that grew tiresome, however, their actions metamorphosed into vandalizing parking meters in the abandoned Ft. Myers downtown. From there, they graduated to smashing car windows.

It's amazing just how much power one youth can wield over others in shaping their mindstates and actions. Fifteen years to the day after the Lords of Chaos came to be, Dr. Valerie Ulene, awardee of MD and Masters of Public Health degrees from Columbia

University, would note in a dispatch to the *Los Angeles Times*, "The influence that friends exert over one another as teenagers is clearly powerful and, far too often, undesirable. Unhealthy behaviors can be almost contagious among kids this age."

Contagious—a word usually associated with infectious disease. And like an epidemic, the miscreance committed by Chris, Derek, and Pete at Kevin's prompting would only spread. After car windows came looting: on several occasions, the boys broke into convenience stores and truck cabins to steal items they didn't even want. They later blew the locks off of 18-wheelers parked behind a local grocery store; once opened, they lit the dry goods and foodstuffs inside on fire.

As they watched that semi trailer burn, a taste for arson was born. The scope of their rampage grew. That same night, they burned down a restaurant. Then a construction site. Then a Baptist church activities bus, and as if merely targeting it to begin with weren't enough, they desecrated a Bible they found on board and used it for kindling.

Quickly, things had gone out of control. And nobody seemed able to stop them from delving deeper into mayhem—until, that is, they ran into Mark Schwebes.

•

Mark Schwebes was the leader of the Riverdale High School band. He was also a former US Marine. Growing up in Long Island, NY, Schwebes had shown prodigious interest in both music and his country, and not long after graduating Cypress Lake High School, he joined the Marine Corps, playing trumpet in the Marines Corps Marching Band throughout his tour of duty.

After completing his service, Schwebes earned a degree in music education from Florida State, and from there, he began a career as a school music director. Though he'd left the Marines for civilian life, he never gave up a number of his military habits. He kept himself trim, fit, and neat at all times. His clothes and hair were just so. And every time he left his post, he always swept the grounds to make sure they were clear. This meant that as he left Riverdale High on April 30th, 1996, at around 9 p.m. (at the tail end of an ice cream social), he found himself face-to-face with a few loitering kids. They were members of the self-styled Lords of Chaos—and some of them were his students.

The local media had begun to report on the goings-on of these theretofore unknown miscreants, and while it stung the boys to have to remain anonymous, they loved collecting the clippings about their rampages. Every time they went out for a night of mischief, they pushed the envelope ever further, as propelled by anger and lawless mayhem as they were by notoriety. First there was the destruction of public and private property—adolescent boys seeking to vent some testosterone and show their dominance. Next came theft, then burglary, and when that proved not enough, the boys graduated to structure fires. Both law enforcement and the media were shocked in hindsight by how quickly these high-school students—to all members of the community, seemingly good kids—graduated from minor vandalism to major felonies. And yet, even after committing arson, the boys were still not satisfied. After burning the truck, the restaurant, the construction site, and the bus all in one night, the next weekend, the boys destroyed a landmark Coca-Cola bottling plant just off US-41 in Ft. Myers' downtown, paying sick homage to the Oklahoma City bombings by detonating homemade explosives in the plant on the one-year anniversary of the Unabomber massacre.

They ruined the historic building, causing over $100,000 in damage. To the boys' minds, that was funny—even more so because they fashioned the improvised explosive device that they used to burn down the Coke plant inside a two-liter bottle of Pepsi.

Still, the very next weekend, the Lords of Chaos went at it again, this time focusing their anger not on buildings or cars, but on people. Emory Lewis was the owner of the Alva County Diner, where Derek Shields worked; he was also Derek's family's landlord. Derek didn't like Emory, he didn't care for how Emory lorded his financial hold over the family, and he especially disliked the way Emory called his mother low-class, deriding her as white trash in the wake of a car accident that had claimed the life of Derek's beloved older brother. In retaliation, Derek's friends and gangmates Pete Magnotti and Kevin Foster robbed Lewis at gunpoint, carjacking him and threatening to kill him as well.

Still, neither parents nor classmates noticed a change in the boys. Cute girls were calling up Pete's house, asking the tender teenager for rides. But just four days later, on April 30, Mark Schwebes would come between the boys and their fun, and that would be the end of everything.

•

By the end of April, the fledgling gang they'd started had grown to be the central focus of the boys' lives. Charismatic Kevin Foster had even gone so far as to rename them all. Chris Black, the tubby computer nerd, was now SLIM. Pete Magnotti, the artist who worked the counter and grill at Hardee's, was now FRIED. Derek Shields, whose family lineage was part Italian, was now MOB.

And Kevin? Kevin was GOD. And heaven protect anyone who stood in his way. Kevin's mother certainly didn't. The first adult to do so at all, in fact, was Mark Schwebes.

On April 30th, Kevin and the boys stormed into a local Dillard's, attempting to set off smoke bombs inside the department store to provide a diversion while they shoplifted clothes. When their incendiaries failed, they moved along to their own high school, Riverdale, where they began to vandalize the auditorium.

That's when Mark Schwebes caught them.

He was doing his nightly drive around the school—the pool, the gym, the auditorium—and he noticed the small posse of kids huddled in the darkness around a payphone. The payphone itself no longer worked—it had been vandalized. Schwebes looked closer, and he saw that the kids, some of whom he recognized as students, carried metal staplers, canned peaches, a fire extinguisher: the perfect heavy projectiles to break a couple windows.

One was wearing gloves, despite the sweltering dampness of the South Florida air. As he questioned them as to why they were hanging around a broken phone in the middle of the night, another took off running.

That was more than Schwebes needed. He confiscated the boys' things and put them in the front seat of his Ford Bronco. He also told them to expect a call to the office from the school police the next morning.

They watched his taillights flicker as he drove away. Chris—the quiet, shy computer nerd—bit his lip in anger, and then spoke ten little words that would dramatically alter the course of their lives.

"Tomorrow is a school day. He's got to die tonight."

Was he kidding? It wasn't clear. But it didn't matter, because to Kevin, it was no joke. Some of the other boys went home, but Kevin went into overdrive. He didn't want to get into trouble, and the very thought of Schwebes reporting what he knew sent him into a frenzy. He took Chris back to his house, and called Pete, who came over as well, and together, they loaded his shotgun.

As for Derek, he was conflicted. He was *in* the band, and he *liked* Mr. Schwebes. On the other hand, his friends had stood up for him—they had assaulted and carjacked his asshole landlord and boss on his behalf.

Derek left Riverdale High, drove home and sat in his driveway. He was pulled in both directions, debating what to do, trying to figure out whether or not he should just go inside and forget the whole thing.

It was not an easy decision, but at last, he made up his mind. He twisted the key in the ignition, pulled back onto the street, and headed straight for Kevin's house.

•

Years later, TV newsman Keith Morrison would interview Derek on *Dateline*.

Morrison: What sort of person is he?

Derek Shields: Double personality, the way I looked at it. In front of most people, he looks like an innocent little kid you know with intelligence and all. [But] if you see the dark side, he's a psycho.

There was a lot to his assessment. Indeed, Kevin was a chameleon, adept at becoming whomever his company wanted him to be. He was a leader and a dropout, a shop-owner and a violent felon, and in short order, he was able to convince the other three teen boys that killing Schwebes was the only way forward.

They loaded into Derek's car and headed towards Schwebes' house, the address gleaned from Information. En route, the other boys timidly tried to convince Kevin to turn back. Kevin wouldn't hear of it.

"Shut up," he said. "I don't want to hear it no more. We're gonna kill him, and if I don't, I'm gonna kill you guys, because someone has to die tonight." That shut them up indeed, and the only other noise made for the rest of the ride was a dirge Kevin made up and sung to himself, a twisted riff on an old Christmas carol:

> *"You better watch out, you better not cry,*
> *You better shut up and prepare to die.*
> *Kevin Foster's coming to your house."*

Just after 11:30 p.m., the boys pulled up to Schwebes' duplex. Derek walked up to the door and knocked; Kevin trailed him with a shotgun. When Schwebes answered, Derek ducked out of the way, and Kevin fired.

Schwebes died before he hit the ground. The boys sped off, returning to Kevin's house to debrief themselves about what they'd just done—all save Pete, who hurried home.

He'd just broken curfew, and he was worried about being out too much later.

•

Amazingly, the boys were not immediately caught or even suspected of having been involved. There was no money missing, nor did Schwebes' residence seem to have been disturbed, so police believed only a jealous ex-lover, or perhaps a spurned former friend, could have killed the former teacher. The boys grew cocky as they read the media reports of law enforcement barking up the wrong tree, and they began to plan ever more horrid crimes—more hateful crimes. They also began to brag. They'd arm themselves, they decided, head over to Disney World on the upcoming high-school Grad Nite, and steal characters' costumes and wear them. This would allow them to travel through the park undetected, shooting any minority patrons who crossed their paths.

They'd graduated even from murder, it seemed, to hate crimes. To realize their idea, though, they'd need the money to buy a stockpile of ammo. They hatched another plan, this one to hold up the Hardee's where Pete worked so they could buy enough bullets and shells to finance the killing spree. They told people about what they had done, and what they would do—first, boasting only to other, minor fellow members of the Lords of Chaos, but then to those guys' friends, and their girlfriends…and finally, someone called the police.

It took little time for police to determine that the info they received was real. In short order, cops staked out Kevin Foster's house, and when the boys loaded their trunks with weaponry to knock over the Hardee's, they struck. They caught the boys armed—including with Schwebes' murder weapon, still bearing Kevin's prints—and charged them all with criminal conspiracy and murder.

Investigators had no trouble figuring out exactly what had happened at the Coke plant, or at Dillard's, or at Schwebes' house, or at the school. The question that stumped them was: why did these young boys start this club to begin with? Boredom? Rejection? Lack of supervision? Some combination of all three? They never did get a satisfactory answer—no one could explain it. With the exception of Foster, who'd dropped out, they were just a month away from graduation. One had even earned a full-ride college scholarship! But now, such a future could never be.

Pete Magnotti pled down and got thirty-two years. Black and Shields confessed to their roles as well, and both earned life sentences. And Kevin? Despite it all, Kevin Foster refused to confess. He took his case to trial, was found guilty, and was condemned to death row.

In an interesting twist, Kevin Foster kept trying to play God, even behind bars. He convinced his mother—and very nearly, a journalist who wrote about his case—to try to take revenge on all his former high school gangmates, the ones whose testimony he felt sealed his fate. He convinced his mother to lure them, one by one, to an abandoned part of Fort Myers, and then, using one of his guns, murder them each in succession.

To the best of Kevin's knowledge, he'd turned the journalist as well. In fact, the writer was going to meetings with Kevin and Kevin's mother while wearing a wire. With the evidence he provided—handwritten notes from Kevin and his mother, along with taped conversations with each—the DA had little trouble earning a conviction.

Now, Ruby Foster sits alongside her son Kevin in their new clubhouse: the Florida penitentiary. And three quiet, shy, driven former high schoolers sit in a special kind of detention there too, waiting for a bell that will never ring.

CHAPTER 14

—

Sacramento, CA—
Theresa Knorr

When criminologists attempt to classify and explain the actions of psychopaths, they frequently delve into the killers' adolescence to search for clues. Did something happen to them in their youths that twisted them so? Were they pyromaniacal, sadistic towards animals, or inveterate bedwetters? Were they exposed to drugs or alcohol, or were they otherwise abused?

When the answer is "yes," we as healthy people tend to sigh with relief. "Ah, that's it," we say. We determine that the problem has been identified, and that we're safe—that such people are far removed from us. But what about when the answer is "no"…what then? How do we respond when we find that someone seemingly normal, seemingly everyday, has taken themselves down a path of such groundless evil?

Theresa Knorr is someone just like that. Theresa Knorr murdered her own children, and not in some crazed, standalone, off-kilt bender, either. That could at least be understood, if not condoned. Rather, Theresa Knorr methodically tortured her kids over the span of years, making multiple attempts on her children's lives before finally, horrifically, succeeding.

•

To all external appearances, Theresa Knorr was, through her early years, just like any other girl. Born Theresa Cross, she was raised in and around Sacramento. She had a sister, with whom she did not get along, and a mother, with whom she did; when her father developed Parkinson's disease and became unable to work, it fell to her mother to leave the home and get a job to provide for the family.

Unfortunately, tragedy struck. In Theresa's early teens, her mother died of heart failure, leaving Theresa's widower father in charge. Unable to work and growing increasingly angry at the world, he was shortly thereafter forced to sell their home and move them all into a small apartment.

Of course, it was only natural that Theresa should want to get away, start afresh. Rather than attempt to earn a scholarship to college, however, or secure a full-time job, Theresa promptly dropped out of high school and married the first person who would have her: Clifford Sanders, a man she had met only months before.

Clifford Sanders was twenty-one when he married Theresa Cross. She was sixteen at the time. If she and Sanders had had sex before they married, it would have constituted statutory rape.

Not that it mattered, though—at least, not in terms of having to worry about a prison sentence. Within two years of their wedding, Clifford Sanders would be dead.

Theresa saw to that.

•

Clifford Sanders barely knew Theresa Cross when he drove her off to Reno for a marriage certificate, and Theresa Cross, for her part, barely knew the world. She had just finished her sophomore year of high school; she'd never had a job, and save the quickie trip to get a license to wed, she'd never been outside of greater Sacramento, still then a provincial town whose population of just under 200,000 ranked it the 63rd-largest city in the country, below Flint, Michigan, and barely above Yonkers, NY, or Worcester, Mass.

"I told him not to marry her," said Clifford's brother Tom, "but when [young men] got their mind set on what they're going to do, they do it."

And so Cliff did. But even with the joy the arrival of an infant brought to the home—a baby boy, whom Theresa named Howard—the marriage began to quickly fall apart. Cliff liked to drink, and it turned out, young Theresa did, too. And when she drank, she got jealous.

"I don't know why," said Cliff's brother Tom. To his mind, there wasn't much to be jealous of. Cliff was a poor unskilled carpenter, and he wasn't much to look at, either. Still, Theresa became convinced that Cliff was looking to leave her. On July 6, 1964, the day after Sanders' birthday, Theresa and her husband found themselves ensconced in one of a seemingly endless string of arguments. As Sanders made his way toward the door, ostensibly to take a walk and cool off, Theresa called out to him.

He stopped and turned around. To his surprise, Theresa stood taking aim at him with a loaded rifle.

He didn't have time to say so much as a word before she fired a round directly into his heart.

•

The trial should have been straightforward. The medical examiner testified that the shot could not have been fired in self-defense— there were no powder burns on the victim; therefore, the bullet had to have been fired from a distance. The shot had also shattered the victim's wrist before lodging in his heart, implying that Cliff Sanders had raised his hands to chest, as if to protect himself. There were the testimonies of Cliff's brother, who said Cliff had never been abusive, and that of Theresa's sister, who affirmed that she was frequently jealous. Lastly, there was the matter of the large life insurance policy—Theresa had made Cliff take it out just weeks before she shot him.

However, to everyone's great surprise, the court returned a verdict of not guilty. This may have been due to the judge's refusal to allow the testimony of Theresa's neighbor, to whom Theresa had snidely boasted just after killing her husband, "No man's gonna leave me." (The woman happened to be married to a sheriff's deputy, and as Theresa had not been apprised of such, the judge ruled the conversation might have constituted a confession obtained under false pretenses.) Or perhaps it was simply the fact that the jury couldn't imagine convicting the fresh-faced eighteen-year-old girl who sat before them, pregnant with her second baby.

Indeed, just before killing her husband, Theresa Knorr had conceived. That left her three months pregnant when she slipped off the hook for the murder of her husband, and him eight months cold in the ground when she gave birth to his last scion: a girl, whom she named Sheila.

•

By all accounts, Theresa's life failed to improve after killing Cliff Sanders. If anything, her moods and behaviors grew only worse. Theresa had learned the worst of lessons: that she could, it seemed, get away with just about any behavior, no matter how reprehensible. She began going out drinking regularly, starting relationships with military men on leave and depositing her toddlers in whomever's care she could wrangle.

After launching a string of these barroom relationships, Theresa found herself pregnant yet again. She promptly married the father, a US Marine named Robert Knorr, and for a time, her growing family actually approached a state resembling happiness. Robert and Theresa moved into a house of their own, having four more children. The first was a girl named Suesan [sic]. Next came a son named William. After that, they had another son, whom Robert named after himself—Robert Jr.—and lastly, another daughter, whom Theresa christened after herself in kind: Theresa Marie, known amongst the family as Terry.

However, just as a dog left alone can seemingly always find its way home, Theresa Knorr slipped back into her old ways. She began accusing her new husband of having affairs, even as, in time, it became ever more clear that she herself was the culprit. After the last of her children was born, she also resumed boozing in earnest.

Once Theresa had driven Robert Knorr away, she met and married a railroad worker named Ronald Pulliam. Their marriage lasted just a year, and it ended when Pulliam got wind of Theresa's continued affairs. A bit farther down the road, Theresa Knorr married yet again: this fourth husband was a Sacramento newspaperman named Chet Harris whom, at the time of their wedding, Theresa Knorr had known for all of three days.

Though her matrimony with Harris were even more short-lived than the previous efforts—within four months, the pair filed for divorce—it lasted long enough for Harris to do two things that left an indelible stain on Theresa Knorr's mind: the first was to begin a supportive, paternal relationship with Knorr's daughters.

The second was to share with Theresa his passing interest in the occult.

Though Harris's marriage to Theresa Knorr didn't work, he did try to maintain the bond he'd crafted with the kids, and this led Knorr, whose propensity toward substance abuse had only continued to grow over this time, to come to two conclusions of her own.

The first was that her blossoming preteen daughters must have somehow grown prettier than she. The second was that they therefore must have been turned into witches who'd gained their good looks through magic.

Alone, borderline alcoholic, clearly unstable, and deeply underemployed—she occasionally worked as a nurse in convalescent homes, but she used the jobs principally as cover to steal prescription medication from both her patients and their onsite care units— Theresa Knorr fell into a horrific pattern.

Days, she spent in a housebound stupor that often involved refusing to get out of bed altogether. Nights, she engaged in frightful fits of child abuse.

According to her youngest daughter, Terry, the damage Theresa Knorr inflicted on her children ranged from verbal and emotional to painfully physical, depending on Theresa's moods. She stamped a wooden two-by-four with the words "Board of Education," and she frequently beat her children with the plank. Even worse, she turned her offspring against one another, often forcing some members of her brood to hold one another down while she beat on that evening's target.

The children never learned to stick up for one another—they couldn't. Even as they were repulsed by their employment in their mother's twisted cruelties, they were also relieved to be spared her wrath.

Theresa Knorr's eldest, Howard, escaped the house as soon as he could. Once he left, he did his best to break off contact altogether. Though this spared him his mother's rage, it also meant he could offer no quarter to his abused siblings, and their lives only grew worse. Theresa began to concentrate her rage ever more virulently upon her growing daughters, whose beauty she found she feared. She would handcuff her girls to the bed and barrage them with punches (or worse, order her sons to do the same); when that failed to temper her anger, she'd hurl steak knives at them or extinguish cigarettes on their backs.

Multiple times, Suesan attempted to run away, but every time she was found, she was dragged back home. No one believed the horrid stories she recounted of what took place in her household, even though neighbors frequently remarked that the Knorr children often appeared skittish and rarely seemed to be let out of the house, even to attend school. Thus, the youths sadly began to accept the beatings as deserved, even normal.

"When they would ask us questions," young Terry Knorr would later admit, "we would say that our mother did not abuse us. We as kids...had gotten used to it, and thought it was the way that everyone got into trouble."

As her alcohol abuse and lifestyle caused her health to continue to deteriorate, Theresa Knorr's rages spiraled ever further out of control. She gained weight, and she blamed the change in her body not on her drinking and immobility, but on spells cast on her by Suesan and Sheila. Thus, she began to force-feed her daughters, hoping that making them eat pot after pot of macaroni and cheese—as many as four in a sitting—would make them gain weight and somehow even the score. When that didn't slake her anger, she took to threatening her girls with a loaded firearm, taunting them repeatedly that she'd shot someone once before and would happily do it again.

Finally, on a hot day in the middle of 1982, the taunts ended. That was the day Theresa Knorr took a derringer pistol and acted, shooting her daughter Suesan in the chest.

•

Their mother had something in her right hand, hanging limply down by [her] side...it was a silver pistol with a black plastic handle.
—Wensley Clarkson, *Whatever Mother Says...*

Sheila and William were out that day, but Robert and Terry were eyewitnesses to the carnage. Their mother and their sister, arguing as ever. Light seeping in through the orange blinds thumbtacked over all the windows. An accusation. An apology. And then, a gunshot.

The youngest Knorr children saw it all. Suesan, shot, backed away blindly, blood pouring out of her rib cage. She fell backwards into the bathtub like in a movie, her limbs splayed in every direction. Her hands went to the hole in her chest, then to the walls, then back to her wound. There was blood everywhere—in the tub, on the tiles, and all over Suesan's blouse. They didn't know that a person could bleed so much.

And yet, somehow, Suesan didn't die. Theresa employed her medical training to treat the trauma, and in time, Suesan—miraculously—stabilized. Which is not to say that to say that she received a high standard of care: on the contrary, Theresa Knorr left her daughter confined to that bathtub for weeks, and any time Suesan felt the call of nature, she simply had to make waste where she lay. Suesan's siblings were charged with bringing her food from time to time and turning on the spigot to wash her bodily wastes down the drain. Theresa herself administered antibiotics, changes of dressings, and pain relievers, all stolen from her employers, but that was as far as she was willing to go to try to coax her daughter back to health. Going to the hospital, even to remove the bullet lodged near Suesan's back, was entirely out of the question. That would invite questions, and likely the police. Theresa had been taken to court for shooting someone before, and she wasn't about to allow that to happen again, even if it did mean the death of one of her daughters.

As fate would have it, it eventually did.

•

*After spraying out most of the flames, he could make out a smoking
figure laid out as on a funeral bier...
"It looks like a mannequin," she said.
"No," Eden said grimly. "It's a body."*
—Dennis McDougal, *Mother's Day*

•

Over the years following the shooting, Suesan Knorr became only
more beautiful, leaving Theresa Knorr to grow ever more crazed,
ever more hateful, and ever more irrationally convinced that her
daughter, now seventeen and nearly legally independent, had made
a pact with the devil. Suesan's mere presence became a reminder
of all that Theresa no longer was, and Theresa wanted her gone.
So when Suesan asked her mother for the money to buy a one-way
ticket to Alaska, promising that she'd disappear and never trouble
her again, Theresa was gladdened—just that day, after all, she'd
thrown a pair of scissors at her daughter like a dagger, lodging the
blades in her flesh—but at the same time, she was wary.

Theresa's hesitation stemmed not from concerns about Suesan's
well-being in the wilds of Alaska; rather, her reserve traced to the
bullet still lodged in Suesan's back. What would happen if one day,
her daughter got it removed? Then forensics might be able to trace
it back to the derringer and use it as evidence against her. Hate
and jealousy aside, there was no way Theresa was willing to let
her daughter walk out into the world in possession of evidence
that could tie her back to a crime.

Eventually, Theresa offered a compromise. She would see her
daughter off, provided that Suesan first allowed her to retrieve the
bullet from her body. Foolishly, Suesan agreed, and Theresa prepped

her daughter for surgery in the best fashion she could manage. As a stand-in for anaesthesia, Theresa plied Suesan with pills and whiskey. Once the girl had passed out, Theresa passed an X-Acto hobby knife to her son Robert—then only fifteen years old—and told him to go ahead cut the bullet out.

With no medical training, Robert did as his mother commanded, slicing through his sister's skin and shoulder blade to try to coax the bullet free. He pulled away layer after layer of her muscle, tearing away with his bare fingers. Though he was able to remove the evidence as his mother insisted, it would be a far cry to call the surgery a success.

Suesan didn't wake up for a day. When she came to, she was in agony. She cried out in constant pain; the wound didn't heal, and Theresa's stolen antibiotics didn't seem to help. She developed septicemia and a fever, and she eventually became unable to even keep down nutrients. It became clear that Suesan would die without medical attention, but Theresa remained unmoved.

"What do you want me to do about it?" Theresa said when Terry, the de facto nurse, told her mother about her sister's worsening state. "If I take her to the doctor, I'm gonna go to jail." Shaken by the prospect of nearing such a fate again, Theresa Knorr selected another option: she forced her sons Robert and William to tie Suesan up and stuff her into the trunk of the car. Then, Theresa drove Suesan and all of her belongings out to an empty roadside turnout deep in the forested mountains of Squaw Valley.

She piled her daughter and all her things into a pyramid in the dirt. Then, she made her son William light a match.

The autopsy showed that Suesan was still alive while she burned.

•

"The abuse that my sisters and I were subjected to by my mother and brothers, no living soul should have to endure . . . The trouble with these abusers is that they make you feel like you are the one that is in the wrong."

—Terry Knorr

•

It's hard to imagine that things could have gotten any worse in the Knorr household after Theresa forced her underage sons to participate in the gruesome murder of their sister. But somehow, they did.

With Suesan out of the picture, there remained only one target for the worst of Theresa's rage: her oldest daughter, Sheila. Theresa still beat them all, of course, but William and Robert were boys, and Terry was too young to seem to Theresa to be a threat. Sheila, by contrast, was lithe and beautiful, and as Theresa—now completely out of work and housebound—continued to deteriorate, her jealousy flared out of control.

Short of money, with four kids living at home and no job, Theresa forced Sheila to turn to prostitution, demanding that Sheila sell her body and bring home every penny she made to support the family. Sheila, all too cognizant of what fate had befallen Suesan when she tried to assert herself, meekly complied—but even that didn't temper Theresa Knorr's fury.

Less than a year after architecting the murder of her daughter Suesan, Theresa Knorr again decided she'd had enough. One day after her daughter came home from turning tricks to keep the other children fed, Theresa accused Sheila of having contracted an STD and passing it along to her via the toilet seat. Sheila swore it wasn't true, but Theresa punished her all the same, locking Sheila in a closet and telling the other kids they were forbidden from bringing her food or water until she atoned.

Theresa kept Sheila in there for an hour, then a day, leaving her there well past the point of fatigue, dehydration, and illness. Another day passed. Then another. Then another. Never once did Theresa open the door to check on her daughter's health.

Theresa Knorr kept her daughter Sheila locked in that closet until she died. And then she kept her corpse in there for three more days for good measure, until the stink became too much to bear.

With yet another one dead, Theresa Knorr turned to the three children she still had at home, the ones she hadn't driven off or killed. Robert and William—her boys, her little hatchetmen—she made seal Sheila's corpse in a cardboard box and dump it near the airport, a Jane Doe for the county to dispose of. And Terry—her youngest, the one daughter she'd not yet murdered—she made douse the apartment in lighter fluid after the family had departed, hoping that the arson would burn down the building and destroy all evidence of who had been there and what Theresa Knorr had done.

In the aftermath, William escaped. Terry did, too.

Robert stayed with his mother. He didn't seem to mind.

•

Despite her unforgivable acts, it would be over a decade before Theresa Knorr would be brought to justice. She moved with her son Robert to Las Vegas. When they ran out of money, she goaded him into robbing a bar at gunpoint. When he killed the bartender during the heist and found himself thrown in jail, she decamped to Utah, where she retook her maiden name and found room in a boarding house, paying her way by serving as a nursemaid to the owner's mother.

William did his best to forget his youth—but Terry Knorr did not. After fighting through a teenage years spent mostly on the streets, constantly battling substance addiction and, like all her siblings, without a high school diploma to her name, she at last was able to pull herself through her trauma and contact the police. As an adult now, her revelations about her mother's wanton abuses were taken seriously. And thanks to the information she was able to provide about theretofore unidentified corpses, Theresa Knorr was able to be charged with murdering her daughters, Suesan and Sheila.

Theresa Knorr attempted to fight the case, at first. She changed her plea, however, when she learned that, to her surprise, Robert and William had offered quite willingly to testify against her.

•

In examining the life of Theresa Knorr and her children, a sad truth comes to light: though all the Knorr children were desperately abused, they remained, in their own way, heroic. Unlike their mother, who visited these crimes upon them, they found the will within—as best they could, anyway—to preserve their humanity.

In 1995, Theresa Knorr was convicted of two counts of murder. She was sentenced to two counts of life imprisonment, with the possibility of parole at age eighty-one, should she live that long.

Regardless, she has outlived all her daughters—Terry Knorr died in 2011, just forty-one years old, the victim of health complications from her years of abuse.

Robert Knorr is in prison. William is in therapy. Howard is estranged from his former wife, though he perhaps has had it easiest life of any of the Knorrs. The three brothers do remain in contact, though they agree that no matter what, they will never again discuss their mother.

CHAPTER 15

Raleigh, NC—Carlette Parker

The Springmoor Retirement Homes is a sprawling, well-manicured village for seniors in Raleigh, North Carolina. Its five-hundred-some residents run the gamut of older citizens: some need assisted living support, some require consistent medical attention, and others remain wholly independent individuals, even well into their eighties and nineties.

Springmoor resident Alice Covington was just such a go-getting older type. If Covington was a retiree, it was in name only. Her friends described her as spry and vivacious, and though she too lived in the Springmoor planned community, she was as energized and put-together as anyone had ever seen. She ran a de facto convenience store in a Springmoor common area, buying snacks and dry goods at the local supermarket and reselling them to folks who had grown unable to drive to town on their own. She kept her own books, did her own shopping, knew seemingly everybody, and was, for an octogenarian, quite an entrepreneur. Everyone who knew her held her in high esteem.

For a long while, Covington's friend Charles Holtz could match her every step of the way. Of course, time waits for no man, and eventually, Holtz came to realize that though he wasn't enfeebled, he wasn't as strong as he'd once been, and he needed someone trustworthy and understanding to help him take care of himself and help complete the day-to-day tasks of living. When that happened, he called Healthmate Home Care.

Despite its name, Healthmate Home Care wasn't an organization that provided health care directly—it was more of a local nursing assistant agency, matching caregivers to those in need almost like a dating service. When Holtz called, Healthmate matched him with an employee of theirs for a number of years whom they highly recommended: Carlette Parker.

At outset, the match appeared to be a good fit. Parker—a married, thirty-four- year-old North Carolina native—seemed to Holtz to be a caring, skilled home health assistant. Like Parker, she was positive and well liked, and she came with years of experience. That's why it was so surprising that on the morning of Tuesday, May 12, 1998, witnesses swore they saw a woman matching Parker's description—young, African American, heavyset—getting in a physical altercation outside a Kroger grocery store with eighty-six year-old Alice Covington.

Odder still was that that was the next time anyone saw Alice Covington, she was propped up in her own car, slumped alongside the steering wheel, a copse of trees standing guard over her corpse.

•

It was two days after her disappearance that Covington's body was discovered—May 14th. Her car, oddly, was found well out in the middle of nowhere, parked fifty yards into the middle of a field off a minor dirt road. The first responders to the scene guessed she'd had a heart attack, but as detectives began to investigate, they found that the particulars just didn't add up. If she'd had a coronary, wouldn't she have swerved off the street, not glided to a stop and turned off her ignition? And what was she doing miles away from her home and her routine?

Next, there was the matter of Covington's clothes. When found, she was wearing a color-matched tracksuit, as many little old ladies do—but underneath her jacket, she wore a bra but no top. That might be a fine look for a club-hopping teenager, but for an eighty-six-year-old?

Lastly, there was another matter: financial. The day she'd disappeared, the old woman had cashed a $2,500 check at a drive-up teller at a First Union Bank in tiny Smithfield, NC, quite far from where her body was discovered and some forty miles away from her home. Forensics suggested that Covington had likely died on that date and while her body was in her car, the money was not—where could it have it gone?

The next day, Carlette Parker voluntarily visited the local precinct to talk to the police, though she had never worked as a home health care aide for Covington. She did it because she was a friend of Covington's, she said—indeed, Parker thought of Covington as an equal. Though they had run into one another in the Kroger parking lot, they didn't fight, Parker said—far from it. They never fought. They got along so well, in fact, that they had a business relationship: in late April, Parker claimed, Covington had written her a check, an interest-free loan for Parker's side business of doll-making. Coincidentally, it was in the amount of $2,500.

For quite a while, Parker gladly and willingly answered all the investigators' questions—though of course, she apologized that she didn't think she could be very helpful. She'd been busy throughout the time between Covington's disappearance and the discovery of her body. On Tuesday the 12th, she'd been out to dinner with her family, celebrating her sister's birthday, and she spent that evening in a motel with her husband. A motel? They didn't live together anymore, but they were trying to reconcile, she admitted sheepishly, and she thought that spending time somewhere new with one another might rekindle their spark. And as for the next intervening day, Wednesday the 13th, she had spent the night in her trailer park with friends, gossiping over wine coolers.

The picture Parker painted to the police was one of a happy and concerned healthcare professional. A little déclassé, perhaps, what with the cheap booze and the motel liaison, but on the whole, a good and well-meaning sort.

When investigators began digging into Parker's past, however, a completely separate story started to emerge.

•

Carlette Parker was indeed well-regarded professionally. She was a licensed and (for all anyone could tell) competent nurse. That said, she was far from a good woman. Detectives looking into the case quickly found that Carlette Parker carried with her a record—a criminal record.

Three years earlier, in the Raleigh suburb of Garner, Parker had pled guilty to embezzling money from an elderly female in her care. In fact, Parker had stolen nearly $44,000—all in the form of checks she had forged from the account of eighty-five-year-old Catherine Stevenson—before being caught.

In the end, Parker pled guilty to sixteen counts of forging unauthorized withdrawals while in Stevenson's employ—each instance totaling just about $2,500. Despite the gravity of the charges, Parker received a sentence of only four years' probation. She received no jail time, and what's more, she was not in any way stripped of her nursing assistant's certification. However, as a condition of her sentencing, Parker did have to provide restitution on the money she stole. She was put on a monthly payment plan, with the proviso that if she missed her payments, it would be considered a violation of her probation, and she would be sent to prison.

At the time of Covington's disappearance and death, Parker was about $4,000 behind in those payments.

All of this information was news to investigators. It also came as a shock to Charles Holtz and the entire staff of Springmoor. Nobody at the retirement village could believe that the seemingly benign and caring Parker could have done such a thing.

However, there was one group of people who were in no way surprised: Healthmate Home Care. The matching agency that had brought Parker into contact with Holtz and eventually, into Covington's circle had known all along that Parker was a convicted criminal, one who'd preyed on the elderly in the past. They simply didn't disclose that information to Holtz.

Jesse Goodman, the director of the healthcare professional registry for North Carolina at the time, noted that such a situation was all too common. "The primary allegation we receive," said Goodman, "is misappropriation of property, or fraud." Agencies like Healthmate were required to perform background checks—and Healthmate did, in fact, perform one on Parker—but past convictions were not necessarily a disbarment from future employment. What's more, though Parker had indeed informed Healthmate of her felony conviction, no laws existed requiring Healthmate to pass that information along.

When Charles Holtz finally did learn about Parker's history, he was stunned. And when investigators learned about it as well, they began to have deep suspicions regarding the carefully-crafted docile and helpful image of one Carlette Parker.

•

Conversations with Alice Covington's relatives and friends consistently provided the same feedback: in addition to her seemingly limitless reserves of energy, she'd boasted two other traits particularly well-suited to a small, independent businesswoman: she was both parsimonious and a fastidious bookkeeper. As they sorted through the deceased Ms. Covington's belongings, police detectives found support for those words. She never wrote large checks, save for rent, and she maintained a running tally of her accounts in a ledger in her checkbook. She used the old-style kind of checks that came with stubs for logging all the pertinent data on the side: pay-to information, check value, and the like. When filling out those checks, she registered every transaction she made.

And yet, there were anomalies. The first had to do with the late-April $2,500 check that Carlette Parker claimed Covington had given her as a loan for her business. For starters, it had been taken from the very back of the checkbook—there remained a number of unused checks in sequence before Covington should have ever reached that one. What's more, it was unlogged, as was the May

12th check for $2,500 made out directly to cash. For those two unusually large withdrawals, there was no data listed in in the stub ledger at all.

As it happened, that large withdrawal from the date of Covington's death didn't stand out only to investigators. A bank teller at the Smithfield branch of First Union recalled the transaction as well—mostly, she said, because it had been so odd. It had indeed occurred at the drive-thru teller window, and a large, young African American woman had been driving the car. She'd passed over Covington's ID, bank card, and the signed check, while Covington sat, unmoving, in the front seat.

At the time, the teller assumed that the old woman who lay against the passenger's side window must have been taking a nap. All the same, she remembered the incident well enough to assure police that Parker had been behind the wheel of the car, and it had been Parker to whom she'd handed the cash.

That same day, the coroner came back with an autopsy report. Despite first responders' initial suspicions, Alice Covington didn't seem to have suffered a coronary. There was excessive fluid in her lungs—so much that it seemed most likely she'd drowned. And though she had been found behind the wheel of her car, in a field, she had also suffered substantial bruising around her face, neck, hands, arms, upper back and shoulders, consistent with self-defense wounds. What's more, there was a little residue stain of unclear origin on the tracksuit jacket Covington was wearing, which didn't seem to comport with her fastidious, sharp nature.

There were also two small puncture wounds in Covington's neck.

In short order, detectives decided to bring Carlette Parker back in for questioning, and they weren't asking: they were telling. This time, Parker brought an attorney along—and this time, her responses were markedly different.

·

"This is going to sound far-fetched," Carlette Parker told police, ignoring any legal advice not to speak. And truly, the revised tale she spun for detectives beggared belief. Under questioning, Parker claimed that the timeline of events of Tuesday, May 12, 1998, proceeded as follows:

She and Covington had indeed argued in the parking lot of the local Kroger. More than that, they fought. Parker then drove Covington's car forty miles down multiple highways to cash a check on Covington's behalf, but only because Covington asked her to—this, even though there were many branches of First Union Bank far closer by.

After drawing out the $2,500, Covington went with Parker to Parker's trailer to keep her company while she got ready for her family dinner. Parker claimed that she then drew a bath for herself, while Covington sat on the toilet—and when Parker left the bathroom for a moment, Covington slipped off the toilet, fell into the tub, and drowned.

In short, Parker admitted that she'd been deceitful earlier and that she had indeed been there when Covington died—but she continued to claim she hadn't killed the older woman. When investigators asked why Parker—a trained home health care worker—hadn't tried to resuscitate the elderly woman or even dial 911 when she found Covington face down in the bath, she shook her head.

Her past wouldn't let her, she said. The people at Springmoor might not have discovered her history, but police surely would. If she were placed at the scene of an elderly person's death, people might think she had been responsible, and she feared she would surely lose her license. So instead, Parker claimed, she stripped Alice Covington's corpse naked, washed and dried her clothes in the laundry machine, then dressed her again. She then proceeded to stick the body in the trunk of her own car, drive to her sister's party, have sex with her estranged husband in a motel, wake up the next morning, drive back to her trailer, move the body from the trunk of her own car into Covington's, then drive out into the middle of nowhere, find a nice shady glen for Covington's remains, prop Covington—all eighty-eight pounds of her—behind her steering wheel, and walk to a gas station, where she was able to call a cab home. Then, after returning to her trailer, where a woman had died the night before, she drank wine coolers until the next day, when Covington's body was found. She did all this, she said, despite having had nothing to do with Covington's death.

Police detectives believed some aspects of Parker's story, particularly the first part: it sounded far-fetched. Actually, everything that happened *after* Covington's death comported with the evidence. It was the timeline of events *before* Covington's demise that was far harder to swallow.

Investigators presented an alternative possibility, one that asked for a far shorter stretch of the imagination. They theorized that Covington had found out about the stolen check and confronted

Parker. They believed that Parker had subdued Covington—that the pair of puncture wounds found in the old woman's neck by the coroner had likely been caused by a stun gun—and had forcibly taken her back to Parker's trailer, where Parker drowned her.

They posited that Parker had next washed Covington's clothes in an attempt to remove evidence, which might explain why Covington's shirt had gone missing altogether, and they deduced that when Parker had taken Covington all the way to Smithfield, it was so Parker would not be recognized by anyone in Raleigh—and that by that point, Covington, posed upright in the passenger's side of the car, was already long dead.

Detectives got a warrant to search Parker's car. In it, they found a stun gun, with probes that perfectly matched the size, shape and spacing of the puncture wounds in Alice Covington's neck. To their surprise, they also found an open can of pepper spray. They tested the pepper spray as well, finding that the residue it left on clothing matched the indeterminate discoloration found on the trim of Alice Covington's jacket.

That explained why Covington's shirt had been jettisoned: it, too, had likely been stained. Parker hadn't just fought with the eight-six-year-old woman she'd stolen from—she hit her with a stun gun and blasted her with pepper spray, too, before choking her out and drowning her in her trailer park bathtub.

•

Four days after Alice Covington's death—and two days after her body was found—Carlette Parker was arrested for murder. The case was tried as a capital crime, and in 1999, Parker was convicted, making her only the third woman in North Carolina to be sentenced to the death penalty since the US Supreme Court had lifted its ban on Constitutional grounds in 1976.

Yet somehow, that's not where Carlette Parker's story ends.

After Carlette Parker's conviction, agents of the North Carolina State Bureau of Investigation began delving even deeper into her background, going beyond her prior conviction and into the particulars of her other past home health care jobs. They found that in 1996—between her fraud conviction and the death of Alice Covington—Parker was closely connected to still another death.

Detective Chris Morgan of the Raleigh Police Department noted,

> "A ninety-one-year-old lady who lived in downtown Raleigh had been found deceased in her home and—lo and behold!— Carlette Parker was one of two certified nursing assistants who had been helping this elderly lady.

> "We started delving back into the bank records and, shazam! It turns out that several checks that had been taken from her account. Various large amounts of money had been written to none other than Carlette Parker. And the statement [that showed those large withdrawals] would have been delivered the day after her body was found."

That unnamed elderly woman was found sitting up in her bath. Her body was exhumed, and the chief medical examiner found that, even years later, there was still such a substantial amount of water present in the victim's lungs as to rule out natural passing due to old age. A new death certificate was issued for her, with the listed cause amended to read: drowning.

•

Detective Morgan made clear that Parker was one of the most duplicitous, least remorseful killers he had ever seen. "She said, 'I got up bright and early the next day, and I've still got Miss Covington in the back of my car, covered up.'" The detective shook his head as he detailed his recollections of questioning Parker before her trial. Parker apparently continued, "'And her body's actually starting to smell a little bit bad, so I take Miss Covington out of my car and put her back in her car...' And then I start trying to think, "What should I do with Miss Covington's body?"'"

According to criminologists, most women who kill do so in defense, in a situation where they feel their options are limited—generally, in a scenario tied to domestic abuse and/or substance abuse issues. Even if not always defensible, these actions are certainly at least understandable. But Dr. Elizabeth Yardley, Associate Professor of Criminology and Director of the Centre for Applied Criminology at Birmingham City University in the UK, noted that Carlette Parker "is a whole different situation. She is somebody who has killed someone she is only casually acquainted with; she has killed for profit. To me, she's exhibiting the characteristics of a *serial* killer."

Coupled with Parker's earlier work, that diagnosis may indeed hold true. How scary, then, to realize that this particular serial killer spent *years* hiding in plain sight, living in the state capital of North Carolina and working as a trusted home health aide for countless elderly and needy people.

Luckily, that era has passed. Until she is put to death by the state, Carlette Parker will spend all her remaining years behind bars on North Carolina's death row.

CHAPTER 16

—

Park City, KS—Dennis Rader

One of Dennis Rader's happiest moments of his life came at his daughter's wedding. He watched her promenade in her white dress, and he smiled, later wrapping his arm around her and posing for a photo in a beatific reflection of her joy.

One of the BTK Killer's happiest moments came when he murdered Nancy Fox, just six months before Rader's daughter was born. He watched her struggle in her rope, and he smiled, later wrapping her corpse in plastic and posing for a photo in a cruel mockery of her pain.

Dennis Rader was many things. He was a family man. He was a churchgoer. He was a homeowner, a Cub Scout leader, a retired air force sergeant, and a college graduate.

BTK was also many things. He was a sadist. He was a torturer. He was an egotist, a pervert, the single worst killer South Kansas ever saw, and a cipher.

For thirty years, BTK managed to keep the secret of his identity and the truth of his double life a complete mystery to everyone. It wasn't until after he was captured that the truth of his sin was at last revealed: he'd been hiding in plain sight, a twisted smile planted there beneath everybody's nose.

•

It was two weeks after Labor Day, 1986. Stephanie Wegerle, a ten-year-old, had just started going back to school for the start of fifth grade. Vicki Wegerle was at her home on 13th Street, playing piano and tending to her two year-old son, Brandon. Her husband Bill was at work.

Vicki heard a knock on the door: it was a man from the telephone company, alerting her to some problems with the wires and asking if he could test the jacks in the house.

She let him in. Within minutes, he would tie her up to her bed and strangle her with her own pantyhose. He never raped her; he simply delighted in the act of dominance and murder, deriving pleasure from the photos her took of her corpse. He used her car as the getaway vehicle—her husband Bill actually passed it going the other direction as he came home for lunch.

When Bill found Vicki, her body was still warm. No money was taken, and no fluids were found. Young Brandon was fine; at two years old, all he could offer in the way of testimony was, "the man hurt mommy."

There wasn't enough evidence to charge him, but for the next twenty years, almost everyone Bill Wegerle knew—including the local police—suspected him of having murdered his own wife.

The only two people who knew the truth were Wegerle himself and BTK.

•

Dennis Rader was born in 1945, the first of four in a small Southeastern Kansas town. His father, William, was a former

Marine corpsman, and after finding post-war employment with Kansas Gas & Electric, he moved the family to the outskirts of the burgeoning city of Wichita, in an outer borough called Park City.

Dennis himself was at first glance an unprepossessing child. He was an average student; he was a Boy Scout, but didn't excel; he went to the youth group at his parents' church, but he wasn't a leader. Friends said he kept to himself and was quiet.

Inside, though, Dennis harbored demons—and their demands of him were loud. From a young age, Rader developed a macabre interest in bondage that blossomed into fetishes of torture and death. Like many boys of his time, he would watch the Mickey Mouse Club and imagine taking starlet Annette Funicello in his arms and having his way with her. Unlike other boys though, he didn't daydream of seducing the actress: he dreamed of cornering her, tying her up with rope, and raping her.

In time, simply fantasizing about dominance, incapacitation, and violence ceased to be enough. During his teen years, Rader began acting out his desires, trapping neighborhood cats and dogs, trussing them, and then asphyxiating them at his leisure.

To his credit, Rader recognized this was a problem. He knew that what he was doing was sick, and he knew that he was wired all wrong. He attempted, if not to sublimate these desires, at least to hide them so he could fit in. However, he also began to study people who had the same urges as he: serial killers. And over time, he stopped trying to stunt his impulses and instead began to cultivate them.

Serial killers, he learned, established a pattern—a victim type. They took pleasure not just in the kill, but in the hunt, in trawling for victims, scanning the world for potential targets and, upon locating one, fixating. Stalking. Envisioning what completion of the act *might* be like. He began to do the same. He'd watch people from afar with focus and intensity. He'd break into their homes, reveling in the rush the transgressions afforded him.

Rader managed to graduate high school without incident. He tried to go off to college and join a fraternity, but it didn't take—he just couldn't be social like the other boys could. He wasn't disliked, but he was distant, and to him, it was clear: he was different.

As the Vietnam War loomed, Rader decided to drop out and get away, enlisting in the Air Force. Unfortunately, Rader couldn't run from himself, and from Texas to Tokyo, he trawled for imaginary victims. When he retired after four years with the rank of sergeant, he returned home to the outskirts of Wichita, to Park City, marrying a girl he had known from high school.

Life, he found, remained a struggle. He tried to return to college, but he had no aptitude, and a degree was not forthcoming. The economy wasn't strong, and he bounced around from job to job with no real direction.

He wasn't smart. He had no real career path. Worst of all, the fantasies of binding, torturing and killing remained, and now, with little else to look forward to, Rader wondered if the time had come to act on his desires.

January 15, 1974 broke cold and clear in Wichita. By 7:00 a.m., the sun began to cut through the air in sharp lines, the way it does on winter mornings when dawn comes late and snow rests heavy on the ground. Carmen, Danny, and Charlie Otero—thirteen, fourteen, and fifteen, respectively—left their home together and bounded off to school. Joseph Otero stayed a little late getting ready for work, playing in the family room with his youngest—Josephine, age eleven, and Joe Jr., nine—while his wife, Julie, prepared sack lunches: peanut butter on white.

They couldn't know it, but danger lurked just outside. Hiding in the backyard, an unseen man watched his breath rise in puffs as he cut their phone lines. He then sauntered up to the rear door just as one of the children was preparing to let the family dog out into the yard, and he pushed past the kid and inside. Joseph Otero—an ex-military man retired after twenty-plus years in the service—rose immediately to stop him, but the pistol the intruder pulled quickly threw a blanket of quiet across the room.

"I'm hungry," the man said, his almost apologetic. "I need food, money, a car. I'm not going to hurt you, but—I need to get out of here." He said he needed help, that he needed to flee—that he would take these things he needed, and then he would go.

They acquiesced. They believed him.

Joseph rifled through his wallet and gave the man what money he had. Joe Junior, at the man's orders, did put the dog outside, so as not to aggravate the situation.

"I'm going to tie you up," the man said—for safety. So he could stay calm; so nothing unnecessary happened. Again, the family did as they were told, without complaint. They thought it was for their own protection.

Of course, it was not. Once everyone was incapacitated, BTK— Bind, Torture, Kill, as his moniker meant, and as he would come to be known—was in control. He suffocated the father and son. He strangled the mother. And the daughter, he led down to the basement.

"What's going to happen?" she asked. He told her she'd be joining her family soon. The killer hung her from a noose tied around a pipe, and once she was dead, he desecrated her corpse. Then he took some mementos and left the scene for the other children to find when they came home from school that afternoon.

•

BTK later testified that he almost didn't commit his first crime. He was very nearly too scared to see it through. But once he had done it—and once he reflected on how easy it had been—he became certain he was going to keep at it. In fact, it was only three months after the Otero murders that BTK struck again.

> I had many what I call them "projects." They were different people in town that I followed, watched. Kathryn Bright was one of the next targets, I guess… Just driving by one day, I saw her go in the house with somebody else, and I thought, "That's a possibility…" It just was basically a selection process; I worked toward it. If it didn't work, I'd just move on to something else, but in the—in the—my kind of person, stalking and strolling..[sic] you go through the trolling stage and then a stalking stage. She was in the stalking stage when this happened.

He broke into Kathryn Bright's house and sat to wait for her. To his surprise, she didn't come home alone—she was with her younger brother, Kevin. That didn't do much to stop BTK, though: he had his tried-and-true line about being a drifter on the lam, and he had his gun. He would subdue and defuse, and then he would kill. But things didn't go as he planned: Kathryn struggled, and BTK didn't get to strangle her like he wanted to; he had to stab her to death in order to keep her from getting away. Her brother Kevin, too, fought back and escaped from his bonds; BTK shot him twice, but still, he escaped, forcing BTK to flee the scene in haste, sure that leaving a living witness meant it was only a matter of time before he was caught.

But it wasn't. Despite recovering, Kevin Bright was never able to identify the intruder. For a second time, BTK had successfully gotten away with murder.

For the next ten years, BTK sent one taunting letter after the next. He reached out to newspapers, to police, to television stations—he was thirsty for notoriety, for recognition, for fame. He had killed and felt no repercussions, and he wanted to let the world know just how potent and unstoppable he was. "There [is] a psycho running loose strangling mostly women," he lamented. "How many do I have to kill before I get my name in the paper or some national attention?"

He killed for the thrill of it, the sexual rush, but he wanted respect to come as well. He wanted his name to ring out from people's mouths in fear. When that didn't happen, he grew frustrated, and he reverted to focusing on the hunt, stalking and trolling, but not finishing the deed.

•

While BTK was furloughed, Dennis Rader was busy. Not long after Rader married, he completed both an associate's degree in electronics and a bachelor's in administration of justice. He utilized these twin educational pathways to launch a fifteen-year career with the ADT home alarm company, spending most of his time installing security systems that Wichita homeowners bought to protect themselves from criminals—criminals like BTK.

Dennis Rader also fathered two children, and in the years that followed, his urges—the stalking, the trawling—diminished. Rader earned respect at his job, and for a time, at least, he was able to keep his past demons at bay.

And if his compulsions got to be too much for him, there was always the shed out back.

Nobody but Dennis went into the shed behind the Raders' house. He kept it locked, and the kids were too young and his wife too trusting to meddle with it. It was his private place, for him alone. Nobody bothered him there. There, Dennis Rader could unearth his trophies—the hidden treasures he'd kept—and relive the moments that buoyed him most.

It was there that Dennis Rader stashed his victims' driver's licenses. It was there where he squirreled away things he'd stolen from their homes. It was there where he went to relish the details, to revisit his grisly crimes.

In his shed, Dennis Rader could look at photos he'd snapped of corpses. He could wear the underwear he'd stolen from his victims' homes. He could bind himself and pose his body like the others' had been, take Polaroids, and stoke his dark fantasies.

And then, he could lock everything up, go back inside, and be father to his daughter and son, trying to push away into the darkest corners of his demented mind that he, Dennis Rader, was BTK.

•

By the mid-1980s, Dennis Rader was living, to all outward appearances, the archetypal suburban family life. He was involved in both his local church and his son's Boy Scout troop. But the urge to kill had grown strong again, and as it happened, scouting trips provided an excellent cover story. If he waited until everyone was asleep at a campout to slink away, and if he crept back before anyone woke in the morning, he could have an airtight alibi, with nobody to watch him and hours and hours in the dead of the night to work whatever sick mischief he wished.

Twice, Rader picked a target and bound, tortured, and killed her while ostensibly chaperoning his son in the woods. Both times, he mutilated his victims' remains, dressing their corpses up in elaborate bondage after murdering them. As if that were not horror enough, both times he took their bodies to his Lutheran church, snapping photos of their twisted forms as he desecrated both their mortal coils and the sanctity of his own place of worship to satisfy his demonic urges.

Once, after one of the older women on their block fell prey to BTK, his own wife had expressed her concern for their family's safety.

"Don't worry," Rader told her. "We're safe."

To his dismay, Rader was eventually fired from ADT. Customers liked him, but his coworkers complained he was a hard man to get along with—obstinate, haughty, downright disrespectful, in fact. Near-sociopathic in the way he discounted and dismissed the feelings and needs of others. It was a tough blow to be dismissed after fifteen years with the company, but soon thereafter, he got another job, a job with the city—a dream job, in fact, for someone like him: a job in animal control.

In short order, Rader was again rounding up dogs and cats and killing them. Best of all, he was getting *paid* for it. He'd put on his uniform and go out into the field and find small animals to put to death. He did it openly, and for this, he was *praised.* It was heaven.

Sure, some townspeople lamented that he was overly strict, that he was far too willing to put down pets for the most minute of reasons. But he was the dogcatcher, wasn't he? That was his job. And if a few more pooches died than strictly needed to—well, who could blame him for trying to do his best work for the city of Wichita?

•

To his own great surprise, Rader found growing calm and a sense of purpose in his family and professional life as the years went by. Between watching his kids grow up and the satisfaction of power gleaned from an eventual promotion to supervisor—to say nothing of the outlet he'd devised to slake his urges through repeatedly killing lesser animals—Rader for the second time did something serial killers almost never do: he stopped.

From 1991 to 2003, BTK fell completely silent. No cops or media outlets got letters from him. Nobody died, garroted by pantyhose and left bound for detectives to find. It was as though he simply disappeared into the ether, transmogrified from a horror hidden next door into ethereal vapor, a ghost story with which to scare Kansas kids.

But if BTK was dormant, Rader was alive and well—and he was just as thirsty for praise as he had ever been. In 2004, when newspapers began to publish retrospectives wondering whatever became of the scourge of Wichita on the thirtieth anniversary of his first killings, BTK awoke from the depths. His daughter had just married and moved out of the house, and his son had joined the armed forces. Left alone and empty-nesting for the first time since his children were born, Rader felt his hunger for recognition get the better of him.

In March 2004, BTK sent a package to the *Wichita Eagle*. It contained a letter and a number of photocopies, including photocopies of Vicki Wegerle's driver's license and a sketch of the crime scene he'd left at her house that day long, long before. For the first time in nearly twenty years, Bill Wegerle could walk down the street without fearing that passersby looked at him and saw the face of a murderer. But now, there could be no doubt that her killer was still out there—and that he was still lusting for death.

Throughout the following year, Rader continued to send letters and boxes to television stations, newspapers, and police, sometimes mailing them and sometimes leaving them in truck beds or behind road signs for officials and representatives to find. In them, he enclosed ever more detailed sketches of his many crime scenes, and sometimes tangible miniaturizations of his victims, using bound and gagged Barbie dolls as simulacra. As time wore on, he began to develop an imagined bonhomie with Lieutenant Detective Ken Landwehr, the lead Wichita policeman working his case and the man who'd take to the media to issue official responses to the notes and packages BTK proffered.

This simulated level of camaraderie and understanding was key to law enforcement's investigation of BTK—keep him talking, they figured, and eventually, he would make a mistake that would do him in. They were right. Rader was, among other things, a bad speller, and when he wrote he did so laboriously in block letters, for fear that either his handwriting or a typewritten note could be traced. He wanted to communicate in detail, not just with drawings, photos, and twisted voodoo representations of his murders, which presented a limitation. So he asked police, in a missive nearly a year after re-establishing contact, "Can I communicate with a floppy and not be traced? Be honest."

Investigators were stunned. Could this be real? Sure, they told BTK, replying via personal ad in the *Wichita Eagle* newspaper to send it along. "It will be okay."

To their surprise, about a month later, they received from BTK a purple floppy disk with a number of Microsoft Word files, his first digital communique. But this transmission carried a fingerprint that proved far more lasting than the killer understood. A quick scan of the disk's metadata showed that the software on it had been registered to ownership of the Christ Lutheran Church in Wichita—and that the last person to edit the files thereon had been a user named "Dennis." A quick Google search showed that one Dennis Rader was the President of the Christ Lutheran Church Council, and within days, a sample of his daughter's DNA was used to prove that Rader had committed the crimes.

That very week, Dennis Rader was pulled over in his car, in what was framed to look like a routine traffic stop. That traffic stop ended with Rader being asked to step out of the car, however, and put into handcuffs.

Rader surrendered quietly. When he was arrested, Lieutenant Detective Ken Landwehr was on the scene, and Rader is reported to have asked him, "What took you so long?"

•

For thirty years, Dennis Rader was a blight on the city of Wichita. Thankfully, that chapter has come to a close. He was tried for, and confessed to, ten murders in all, their dates stretching across three decades. Sentenced to a minimum of 175 years in prison, he will spend the rest of his life behind bars.

In the aftermath, Rader's wife has divorced him, and his children have broken off contact. His daughter, in particular, has been especially vocal, dismayed that the very man who raised her, walked her down the aisle and tenderly gave her away could have been the same person to perpetrate these gruesome slayings.

As a final denouement, the city government has purchased the site of Rader's home—as well as his garden shed—and bulldozed it, hoping to remove as completely as possible the stain that Rader's twisted mind and actions left on Park City.

For his neighbors, however, and the surviving family members of his victims, that is a process that will take a long, long time.

CHAPTER 17

—

Yorkville, IL—Dennis Hastert

Sometimes when you live a life of crime, it's not the acts themselves that get you—it's the paper trail. That was certainly the case for Al Capone. After killing a few dozen men himself and being responsible for the deaths of hundreds more, running Chicago's bootlegging rackets throughout the Prohibition Era and rigging any number of Illinois public elections, Capone finally went down for the count on a tax evasion charge. Mitch McDeere may have said it best in *The Firm*: "It's not sexy, but it's got teeth." Public Enemy #1 got put away by a few pencil-pushing accountants.

For Denny Hastert, things went much the same way. He lived his sins and got away with them, showing a smiling, beatific face to his neighbors and world as he hid incredibly foul, dastardly acts all the while. But it was his financial deceptions that brought him before the courts and brought his past to light, exposing the depths of his depredation to all.

Hastert never pulled a gun on any of his victims; that much is true. However, the nearly two million American adolescents who've survived the repugnant crimes committed by Hastert and those like him may argue that they were far, far worse than any caper pulled off by Capone.

•

Dennis Hastert was born on January 2, 1942, a blisteringly cold day in the Chicago suburbs. As a kid, he worked in his family's feed store and helped sell eggs and raise their livestock, later working at family-run restaurants and delivering milk for a nearby dairy. He also played football and wrestled, by high school becoming, by his own retelling, something of a student-coach in each.

He also began to grow devout in his proclaimed dedication to Christian values—among them, the Ninth Commandment: Thou shalt not bear false witness. In his own memoir, referencing a teenage boxing match against his friend in which he emerged with a broken nose, Hastert claimed he couldn't lie to his mother about what had happened, despite the fact that he knew he'd be punished.

"I blurted out the truth. I was never a very good liar," he wrote. "Maybe I wasn't smart enough. I could never get away with it, so I made up my mind as a kid to tell the truth and pay the consequences."

After high school, Hastert went to a local college—the first in his family—where he found himself growing ever more interested in both athletics and education. Above his father's protests, he pursued his teaching credentials and got a job at the high school just down the road from his birthplace in Yorkville, a town of fewer than two thousand people. Everybody knew everybody there, and people quickly warmed to Hastert's enthusiasm for teaching social sciences and coaching both his old letterman sports: football and wrestling.

•

It had to be one of the strangest civil filings Judge Robert Palmer had ever seen.

It was a complaint for Breach of Contract between two individuals. This particular claim covered an oral agreement, rather than a written one—always tricky, but not so unusual by itself. What made this claim really stand apart was its specifics. The judge read the lines over and over:

> *Defendant violated the special trust Plaintiff placed in Defendant by sexually molesting and abusing Plaintiff...*
>
> *[Defendant] agreed to pay Plaintiff $3.5 million to compensate Plaintiff for harm caused by [Defendant's] sexual abuse, and Plaintiff gave up any right to sue for personal injuries or seek any public acknowledgement...*
>
> *Defendant withdrew cash from multiple bank accounts in amounts intended to keep the settlement secret...*
>
> *After [Defendant's] numerous cash withdrawals became the subject of Federal criminal charges against [Defendant], [Defendant] breached the Settlement Agreement by failing to pay the remaining amount owed...*

In short, the Defendant had admitted that he'd molested the Plaintiff. And he admitted that he'd at one time agreed to pay the Plaintiff because of those criminal acts of child abuse he'd committed. But since he'd since been caught and exposed, the Defendant wanted to get out of paying what he'd agreed to pay. The plaintiff was suing to collect the hush money he'd been promised by his molester, leaving the judge to decide: what was the Defendant really paying for? Silence, or the lifetime of pain and anguish he'd inflicted on the little boy he'd ruthlessly sodomized years before?

The judge had to decide: was the Defendant being blackmailed by his own victim? Or was he paying damages for the injury that his admitted sexual abuse had caused?

•

Dennis Hastert was proud of being a coach. As he described it, it was more than a vocation: it was a calling. Coaching his high school boys' wrestling team to the 1976 Illinois State Championship "was probably the greatest experience I'd ever had in my life," Hastert wrote, which in hindsight may have felt like a slap in the face to the woman he married. Still, at the time, no one felt anything but admiration for the focused coach who'd happily volunteer to load students into his van and drive them hundreds of miles across the country to wrestling camps—frequently under his supervision and his alone.

He "carried ten or twelve kids in the van each time," according to his retelling. He also removed all the seats, forcing the youths to sit crammed one against another. By his claims, this was to accommodate more room for students' gear. Others might point out that it also normalized them to constant, close physical contact with other males. This may have been good for grooming them into preparation for wrestling, but it was surely good for grooming these pubescent boys for another type of contact, too.

Hastert's was the classic tale of "local boy makes good," and he reveled in keeping true to his Chicagoland roots. Throughout it all, Hastert found himself beset by opportunities for promotions— he was offered a high-paying job as an Assistant Principal, and the University of Illinois came knocking with an offer of the head wrestling coach's position at their collegiate program. But Hastert always found a reason to decline. He just couldn't leave those boys. It wasn't until a seat opened up in the Illinois House of Representatives that Hastert finally did find a reason to break away from his young charges and his hometown: power.

Starting in the 1980s, Hastert spent six years in the Illinois State Legislature. When a political mentor—formerly a colleague in the state house, but by then, a US Congressman—died, Hastert pushed his way into Washington, where he would stay for two decades. He reigned as Speaker of the House for nearly half that time, and his tenure there was marked in particular by two traits: one was to tirelessly direct spending projects back to his county. The other was to ensure that the federal government marginalized gay and lesbian Americans.

While controlling the federal legislative branch, Dennis Hastert actively blocked anti-hate crimes legislation. He also fought ruthlessly to allow employers to openly discriminate against and fire workers based solely on their sexual preference, and he tried to pass a Constitutional amendment banning gay marriage.

News came to Hastert in 2006 that closeted Republican Congressman Mark Foley was engaging in lewd acts with male minors enrolled in the Congressional page program. Utterly disregarding the children being targeted, Hastert attempted to sweep the whole matter under the rug to protect his colleague, the pederast.

When the scandal did break, Congressmen Foley repented and immediately resigned, later beginning life anew as a happy and openly gay man in Southern Florida. Hastert, on the other hand, took a different tack, denying having ever even heard about the matter.

After working to try to shield this child predator from justice, Hastert nonetheless managed to stay on as Speaker of the House for a whole extra year.

It would be quite a long time before anyone could pin anything on old Coach.

•

Dennis Hastert's autobiography, published during his tenure as Speaker, is full of folksy straight-talk. He spends ample time discussing his Yorkville roots and how happy he was to have come of age in a small town, surrounded and beloved by working-class neighbors. What it doesn't detail, however, is how Hastert got rich—and rich he did become. He entered Congress a common middle-class American, true, but he left a very wealthy man.

Hastert earned the majority of his stake by leveraging his political clout to orchestrate an underhanded real estate deal. Interestingly, this deal was decried by the American Enterprise Institute—a conservative think tank otherwise hugely supportive of Hastert's Republican Party—as even worse than anything disgraced Congressman Foley had done.

In the first phase of his scheme, Hastert took out a mortgage to buy a lot of cheap land in the middle of nowhere. He then merged that land into a trust with some friends who owned other, more valuable property nearby. The men agreed to apportion ownership shares in the trust according to acreage, rather than value, leaving Hastert well ahead of where he'd started.

Why were Hastert's companions happy to do this? Because they knew Hastert wasn't finished. As Speaker of the House, Hastert then forced a spending bill through Congress that called for the new construction of federal roadways—and wouldn't you know it, one of them rolled right by his property.

Nobody wanted the highway—not the federal government, not the state of Illinois, nobody—save Hastert, who stood to make out like a bandit. His formerly worthless property was now situated right by a highway, making it suddenly very valuable and allowing Hastert to sell the land at a massive markup. After paying back his loan, Hastert was able to turn his own tiny investment into over $6 million of pure profit—a huge chunk of which came to him directly from the coffers of American taxpayers.

That taste wasn't enough, though. It never is. After leaving Congress, Hastert began peddling his influence and access as a high-salaried lobbyist, earning millions more by twisting his former colleagues' ears on behalf of Big Tobacco, the fossil fuels industry, and for-profit education.

As it turned out, he was going to need all that money quite soon.

•

In 2010, one of Hastert's former wrestlers reached out to him after years of silence. It was not a happy reunion, because back in his Yorkville High School days, Hastert had done the unthinkable to that student: he'd molested him. Even worse, that boy wasn't the only one.

Throughout his time as a trusted educator, Dennis Hastert had targeted, isolated, and serially molested children placed under his care. As a coach and as a Boy Scout Explorer troop leader, he had no trouble finding and selecting new victims. For years, Hastert kept his pederasty from his neighbors, living a double life as a pillar of the community even as he time and again gained a boy's trust and the trust of that boy's family before committing heinous sexual assaults.

He'd molest kids in motel rooms at wrestling meets. He'd stake out a spot outside the locker room shower and pull up a chair to watch. He'd even bring boys on scuba diving trips to the tropics, lavish them with attention and praise, and then sodomize them. It was beyond awful.

Now, years later, Hastert and this grown man talked, discussing the abuse Hastert had perpetrated and how both of their lives had diverged from that point. The former victim explained how he'd suffered severe depression, developed mental disabilities, and found himself unable to cope with day-to-day working life because of the breach.

To his credit, Hastert didn't deny what he'd done—on the contrary, he seemed eager to, in his own way, atone, going so far as to offer to pay the now-grown man for all the pain and psychiatric suffering Hastert had visited upon him. That said, he may well have been less driven by the desire to help his victim than his hope to keep his actions a secret—and at this point, they still were secret, to all but a very few people save his victims and Hastert himself. All the same, Hastert agreed to compensate the man for the crimes he'd committed against him.

And thus began the series of payments that would finally lead to Hastert's unmasking.

•

Along with his anti-gay stance, his enrichment at the hands of taxpayers, and his protection of a child predator, Hastert's time in Congress was profoundly marked by a push to strip citizens of their civil liberties in favor of government oversight. It wasn't just the LGBT community, either—it was everyone. In his zeal, Hastert leapfrogged the 4th, 5th, and 6th amendments to the US Constitution and to help push into place sweeping conservative measures like permitting the indefinite detention of criminal suspects without actually charging them of a crime, and of refusing suspected criminals access to legal counsel.

He also helped provide the US government with broad new powers to track private citizens' financial transfers.

All this meant that when Hastert started making a series of $50,000 cash withdrawals from the war chest he'd built up over the years to send payments his former victim—the boy he'd molested who would grow into the man identified in court papers only as "Individual A"—the Treasury Department began to take an interest.

Somehow, Hastert hadn't considered the fact that he might be surveilled as well, or that the government might notice a man yanking cash from his vaults like Scrooge McDuck on an insane bender.

Once Hastert realized that he had begun to garner scrutiny, did he shy away from his duplicity? Of course not. Instead, he began structuring a new series of withdrawals in dollar amounts just small enough to fall barely below the banking system's mandatory reporting limit. That he might not have gathered that intentionally obstructing his actions from law enforcement oversight was, in fact, a crime in and of itself should not come as too much of a surprise—after all, obfuscating his crimes was something Hastert had by that point been doing for decades.

In the end, it was the financial machinations that brought him down. Regulators noticed that Hastert had begun to make these regular, smaller withdrawals only after he'd been questioned about the larger ones. When a now-curious FBI asked him about whether he was trying to shield his financial movements, he lied to the investigators—and that was the last straw.

Nearly fifty years after he had begun his work in Yorkville High School sowing the seeds of abuse, Dennis Hastert was charged, tried, and found guilty—but not for his plethora of sex crimes. On those, the statutes of limitations had run out, if not the public memory. No, what finally took Hastert down was his illegal structuring of bank transactions to try to hide the fact that he'd committed those sex crimes (and was paying off a victim to keep it mum).

"If there's a public shaming of the Defendant because of the conduct he's engaged in, so be it," said the judge who sat at his trial, finally exposing the double life that this friend and neighbor to the Illinois small-town working man had long led. "Nothing is more stunning than having 'serial child molester' and 'Speaker of the House' in the same sentence."

When the news of his years of rape, molestation, and sodomy broke, Yorkville shied away from its ties with its old favored son. Reporters who covered the story found themselves confronted by a town fearful of both reporters and their former admiration.

Hastert was seventy-nine when he reported to federal prison in Rochester, Minnesota, leaving untold children broken and damaged in his wake. If and when he is released, he will have to register as a sex offender—which, at the very least, means he'll have to stay far away from Yorkville High School.

CONCLUSION

—

All in all, it took me about two years to create this book, from inception, to planning, to research, to writing. When I'd started this project, it was because of the criminals I'd once known—because of the sad undoing of people who had once been close to me. Thinking about the double lives they'd led pointed me toward some of the worst modern Americans I could find: people who'd not only lived as unrepentant criminals, but who held their own hometowns in terror as they kept their secrets. The working title was *Local Boy Makes Bad*. This book was meant to be entertaining, informative, thrilling—hopefully, you found it to be all three. There is something about criminality that leaves us stunned, in both the positive and negative senses of the word: we are horrified, but we cannot look away.

I didn't know personally any of the people I'd planned to detail. This book was to be, and has primarily remainded, a series of case studies on the dregs of humanity and the way our own neighbors can cause harm behind the aegis of their duplicity: they can steal, they can conspire, they can betray, and they can kill. But during the process, as the double lives of people I *did* know became clear to me in the most unfortunate and final of ways, I couldn't help but reflect on practitioners of that other kind of duplicity: people who inflict self-harm. Sociopaths hurt others without regard; addicts become rewired to hurt themselves with that same seeming indifference. Recognizing this forced me to think about the nature of double lives in another, second way.

A friend of mine asked me about these two aspects of the text. Had I created a mash-up, he asked, or a clash-up? In other words, had I bridged worlds; had I developed something more than the sum of its parts by including my own lived experience regarding this related behavior? Or was I trying to jam together two such distinct thoughts that the end product produced more discord than harmony?

I thought about it for quite a while before determining that the topics are indeed part and parcel—one way or another, there's horror on the other side of that blanket. And truth be told, most of us are far more likely to come across an addict next door than a crook or a killer (and thank heavens for that). But criminals tend to be more interesting to read about—they do more. That's why they make the news. Addicts don't. They just live a double life 'til they die. I may be no closer to being ready to support addicts than I was when I started writing—indeed, the people who dedicate their lives to such a pursuit have my highest respect. But at least I know more about them.

For sociopaths, likewise, the same is true in both regards.

•

Day by day, our world continues to change. Consider the case of Joseph Portash. The thug mafia of his time, of *Casino* and *Goodfellas*, is far less prevalent now. There's precious little to be made in protection rackets and gun-toting heists anymore. The real treasure troves these days are all online, all digital; ex-Communist hackers, financial markets: that's where the money is in mischief these days. One need only look at the recent waves of ransomware to confirm as much. And sticking up banks? Forget about it. Tomorrow's Carl Gugasian is living a double life right this minute, locked away in front of the family computer, learning how to program. (That, or he's developing the data analytics skills to stop the likes of the next John Orr or Genene Jones well before they can ever build up a body count.) Even drug dealers these days are moving off of street corners and onto the corners of the Dark Web.

What about Tennessee catfishing queen Jenelle Potter? I poked around Nextdoor, the same online message board she frequented. As far as I could tell, no one else in the state has tricked her own family into murder as she did, but plenty of people there have managed to wreck their homes through opioid addiction. Indeed, opioid possession and distribution rates continue to rise, even as other types of crime recede. Newspapers and nonprofits alike agree: there are now more active opioid prescriptions in Tennessee than there are people who actually live in the state. (What's more, that only covers the *legal* stuff—it doesn't even touch the contraband market.) Can we even wrap our heads around just how widespread that hidden problem must be? Let's not forget methamphetamine, either. As Joe Woodward, Chief Deputy of the Johnson County Sheriff's Department, said to me while lamenting an addiction that's taken Mountain City, Tennessee, in its hold, "That methamphetamine— once you get hooked on it, it's got you for a long time."

Interestingly, in the time since I started working on *Double Lives*, addiction itself has entered the cultural consciousness. Municipalities and states are pursuing legal recourse against facilitators of addiction, and perhaps that may mean that future writers won't find the same source of inspiration I did. I wouldn't mind that. But crime will always be crime, and the secret criminals among us, whomever they may be, will always exist—and they will always keep us turning the page to inform, thrill, and horrify ourselves about what may be lurking just next door, wherever we are.

All in all, it almost doesn't matter what particular horror keeps us up at night, and it doesn't matter what type of double lives the monsters around us may lead. The clock on the nightstand will always say it's time to tuck our ankles in.

ACKNOWLEDGMENTS

—

First and foremost, I'd like to thank my family, who made this possible. To my wife, my parents, my sister, and all my nieces, cousins, aunts, uncles, and grandparents: thank you.

Thank you to every person who spoke to me—most of your names are in the final pages of the book (and to those of you whose names aren't listed, you know why). I thank you just as deeply.

Thank you to my friends and mentors, teachers, and colleagues.

Thank you to my agent, editors, and fellow writers.

Thank you to the organizations, schools, and benefactors who have lent their support both to this project and to my work in general over the years.

Thank you to everyone who endeavors to make their world, their nation, their state, their city, or even their block a better, safer, and more just place to live.

Lastly, thanks to you for reading.

BIBLIOGRAPHY

—

Note: because efforts were made to protect the identities of people not specifically profiled in this book—including my friend Evan—resources that would necessarily identify them have been omitted from this list of bibliographic sources.

Chapter 1: John Orr

Berger, Leslie. "Ex-Fire Captain Charged in 4 Deaths in 1984 Store Blaze." *Los Angeles Times.* November, 11 1994. Print.

Bovsun, Mara. "Chief Arson Investigator in California Town…" *New York Daily News.* July 12, 2014. Web.

Brown, Rhonda and Davenport, Jackie. *Forensic Science: Advanced Investigations.* Cengage Learning, 2012. Print.

"Determining Arson Motives." Intefire.org. Accessed July 2016. Web.

Gray, Chris. Personal interview. 19 July 2016.

Hanly, Pat. Personal interview. 13 July 2016.

Hoffman, Gretchen. "Orr Novel Piqued Author's Interest." *Glendale News-Press.* June 1, 2002. Web.

Keyes, Gary, and Lawler, Mike. *Wicked Crescenta Valley.* The History Press, 2014. Print.

Lucero, Glen. Personal interview. 20 July 2016.

Matassa Mike. Personal interview. 21 July 2016.

"Point of Origin," *Forensic Files*. truTV. 27 October 2004 (Season 9, Episode 21). Television.

US Court of Appeals for the Ninth Circuit—29 F.3d 636 (9th Cir. 1994)—Argued and Submitted July 11, 1994. Decided July 21, 1994.

Wambaugh, Joseph. "Blaze of Glory." *LA Times Magazine*. April 28, 2002. Print.

Wambaugh, Joseph. *Fire Lover*. William Morrow, 2002. Print.

Chapter 3: Carl Gugasian

Caruso, David B. "Prolific Bank Robber to Help FBI." *CBS News*. December, 10, 2003. Web.

"The Friday Night Robber." *Masterminds*. truTV (Canada), original air date unknown. Television.

Krajicek, David J. "How Two Boys Helped the FBI Find…" *New York Daily News*. September 29, 2013. Web.

Merluzzi, Fred. "Broad Mountain Bank Robber." *Pennsylvania Game News*. July 2004. Pub: Pennsylvania Department of Conservation and Natural Resources. Print.

Rodell, Chris. "The Professional: America's Greatest Bank Robber." *Stuff Magazine*. March 2005. Print.

Sanchirico, Chris William. "Evidence, Procedure, and the Upside of Cognitive Error." *Stanford Law Review* 57.2 (Nov. 2004): pp. 291–365.

Slobodzian, Joseph A. "'Friday Night Bank Robber'..." *Philadelphia Inquirer.* December, 5, 2003. Web.

Chapter 4: David Graham and Diane Zamora

American Justice. "Duty, Honor And Murder." A&E, originally aired October 7, 1999. Television.

Bardwell, S.K. "Inmates Who Never Met Say They Want to Marry." *Houston Chronicle.* March 13, 2003.

Buss, David M. *The Murderer Next Door: Why the Mind Is Designed to Kill.* Penguin, April 2006. Print.

Dateline NBC. *"Diane Zamora: 'I'm not a Killer.' "* NBC, originally aired April 8, 2007. Television.

"Former Air Force Cadet Expresses Remorse for 1995 Slaying of Teen." *Denver Post (AP).* February 10, 2008.

"Former Air Force Cadet Gets Life in Texas Teen's Slaying." *CNN. com.* July 24, 1998. Web.

Graham v. State. Court of Appeals of Texas, Fort Worth. No. 2-98-483-CR. October 21, 1999.

Hewitt, Bill. "Sealed in Blood." *People*, Vol. 46 No. 17, October 21, 1996.

Hewitt, Bill and Stowers, Carlton. "To the Bitter End." *People*, Vol. 49 No. 8, March 2, 1998.

Hollandsworth, Skip. "The Killer Cadets." *Texas Monthly.* December 1996.

Meyer, Peter. *Blind Love: The True Story of the Texas Cadet Murders.* St. Martin's True Crime Press, January 1998. Print.

Pierce, Ellise. "Love is a Killer." *Dallas Observer.* October 17, 1996.

Pressley, Sue Anne. "Zamora Accuses Former Fiancé in Slaying of Rival." *Washington Post.* February 11, 1998.

Thompson, Neal. "Friend Says Zamora Told Her of Killing Witness…" *Baltimore Sun.* February 03, 1998.

Thompson, Neal. "Zamora Had 2nd Romance, Academy Friend Testifies." *Baltimore Sun.* February 04, 1998.

Verhovek, Sam Howe. "A Tale of Love and Murder in a Small-Town." *New York Times.* September 10, 1996.

"Zamora Trial: 'Shoot Her, Kill Her'." *CBSNews.com.* February 2, 1998. Web.

Zamora v. State. Court of Appeals of Texas, Fort Worth. No. 2-98-098-CR., 998 S.W.2d 290 (1999). July 1, 1999.

Chapter 5: Andrew Kehoe

Bauerle, Ronald: *The Bath School Disaster.* Ancestry.com. Web.

Bernstein, Arnie. *Bath Massacre: America's First School Bombing.* University of Michigan Press, 2009. Print.

Buhk, Tobin T. *True Crime: Michigan: The State's Most Notorious Criminal Cases.* Stackpole Books, 2014. Print.

Burcar, Colleen. *It Happened in Michigan: Remarkable Events That Shaped History.* Globe Pequot / Rowman & Littlefield, 2011. Print.

Dotinga, Randy. "America's Deadliest School Violence? Not Columbine, but Bath, Mich., in 1927." *Christian Science Monitor.* July 24, 2012.

Ellsworth, Monte J. *The Bath School Disaster.* Self-Published, 1927; re-published by Bath School Museum Committee, 1991. Print.

Lamb, C.E.; Searl, William C; Whitman, Glenn; et al. *May 23–25, 1927 Clinton County, Michigan Coroner's Inquest.* Print.

"Maniac Gave Grim Advice on Picnic." *Youngstown Vindicator.* May 19, 1927: Page 10, Column 5. Print.

Mayo, Mike. *American Murder: Criminals, Crimes, and the Media.* Visible Ink Press, 2008. Print.

"Survivors Recall 1927 Michigan School Massacre." *Morning Edition.* National Public Radio, April 17, 2009. Radio.

Chapter 6: Jenelle Potter

Brooks, Dennis. *Too Pretty to Live: the Catfishing Murders of East Tennessee.* Diversion Books, 2016. Print.

Campbell, Becky. "Update: Mother, Daughter Receive Concurrent Life Sentences in 2012 Mountain City Double Murder; Co-Conspirator Gets 25 Years." *Johnson City Press.* July 8, 2015. Web.

Diaz, Joseph and Valiente, Alexa. "How a Social Media Feud Led to the Murder of a Young Tennessee Couple." *ABC News,* October 9, 2015, Accessed June 21, 2016. Web.

Iwano, Ruth (Ed.) "#Unfriended." *20/20.* ABC. October 9, 2015. Television.

Tennessee Felony Offender Information Listing (FOIL). Accessed June 22, 2016. Web.

Chapter 8: Louis Eppolito

Caruso, Michelle. "I'M GONNA FIGHT TILL DAD'S HOME. Mafia cop's daughter says he's innocent, vows to spend her life saving his." *New York Daily News*. June 11, 2006. Web.

Clifford, Stephanie. "Family of Man Killed by Rogue Detectives Settles Suit for $5 Million." *New York Times*. July 30, 2015. Web.

Dwyer, Jim. " 'Mafia Cops' Get Life, and Their Pensions." *New York Times*. March 6, 2009. Web.

Eppolito, Lou and Bob Drury. *Mafia Cop*. Simon & Schuster, 1992. Print.

Feuer, Alan. "Of Murder, Mob Witnesses and Shouting in the Court." *New York Times*. March 14, 2006. Web.

"The Inside Story of The Mafia Cops Case." *NY Law*. Episode 0917, Dec 21, 2012. New York Law School Media Services.

"Israel Greenwald's Family Awarded $5 Million After Being Slayed By NYPD." *Jewish Political News & Updates*. August 2, 2015. Web.

Lawson, Guy, and Oldham, William. *The Brotherhoods: The True Story of Two Cops Who Murdered for the Mafia*. Simon & Schuster, 2007. Print.

"Mafia Cops." *Sally Jesse Raphael*. 1992. Television.

"Mafia Cops?" *60 Minutes*. January 5, 2006. Television.

Marzulli, John. "Last of NYPD 'Mafia Cops' lawsuits finally settled, bringing total payouts to $18.4 million." *New York Daily News*. August 28, 2015. Print.

McGrath, Ben. "Kiss City." *New Yorker*. May 1, 2006.

UNITED STATES of America, Appellant, v. Louis EPPOLITO and Stephen Caracappa, Defendants-Appellees. United States Court of Appeals, Second Circuit. Docket Nos. 06-3280(L), 06-3396(CON). Decided: September 17, 2008.

Chapter 9: Joseph Portash

Bradley, David. "Property Taxes in Perspective." *Center on Budget and Policy Priorities*. March 17, 2005.

Coombe, William M. "Schmertz Indicted on Bribery Charge." *Nashua Telegraph*. February 6, 1975.

Davis, Tom. "PORTASH: The Fate Of Joe Portash's Widow." *Manchester Patch*. March 22, 2013. Web.

DePalma, Anthony. "In New Jersey, Adult-Village Builder Shifts Gears." *New York Times*. December 25, 1983.

"Joseph S. Portash." *Findagrave.com*. Web.

LeDuc, Daniel. "The Town Joe Portash Left Broke." *Philadelphia Inquirer*. October 14, 1990.

Peele, Thomas. "PORTASH: How New Jersey's Most Crooked Politician Was Finally Caught." *Manchester Patch*. January 4, 2013. Web.

"Schmertz Is Charged With Bribing Portash." Asbury Park Press. February 6, 1975.

State of NEW JERSEY, Petitioner, v. Joseph S. PORTASH. Supreme Court of the United States of America. 40 US 450 (99 S.Ct. 1292, 59 L.Ed.2d 501). March 20, 1979.

Sullivan, Joseph F. "Owner of Celtics Indicted in Jersey." New York Times. February 6, 1975.

Sullivan, Joseph F. "Huge Fraud Case Shaking New Jersey Haven for Aged." New York Times. September 3, 1990.

Sullivan, Joseph F. "7 Ex-Officials of New Jersey Town Are Accused of Looting It." New York Times. March 1, 1991.

"The First Senior Citizen Development in New Jersey Turns 50." Township of Lakewood Website. September 11, 2013. Web.

"Tom Peele." UC–Berkeley School of Journalism. Web.

US Census Data.

Warnet, J.R. and Galioto, Catherine. "25 Years Since Manchester Changed To Nonpartisan Government." Manchester Times. March 27, 2015. Web.

Chapter 10: Genene Jones

Anderson, Teresa H. "Dr. Kathleen Holland, a Pediatrician Who Employed Nurse Genene Jones…" UPI Syndicate. January 26, 1984.

Collier, Dillon. "'Killer Nurse' Genene Jones Back in San Antonio to Face New Murder Charges." KSAT 12 News. December 4, 2017.

"Convicted Baby Killer Set For Early Prison Release." *Crime and Punishment.* CNN. Aired August 20, 2013.

"Convicted Infant Murderer Genene Jones Could Be Set Free In Two Years." *The Source.* Texas Public Radio. Aired June 30, 2016.

"Dark Secrets." *Deadly Women.* Season 2, Episode 4. Aired October 30, 2008.

Davis, Carol Anne. *Women Who Kill: Profiles of Female Serial Killers.* Allison & Busby. 2001. Print.

Di Maio, Vincent, and Franscell, Ron. *Morgue: A Life in Death.* St. Martin's Press, 2016. Print.

Elkind, Peter. "The 'Angel of Death' Nurse Charged with Death of Second Baby." *Texas Monthly,* co-published with *ProPublica,* June 2017. Web.

Elkind, Peter. "The Death Shift." *Texas Monthly.* August 1983.

Elkind, Peter. *The Death Shift: The True Story of Nurse Genene Jones and the Texas Baby Murders.* Viking, 1989. Print.

Forney Jr., Robert B., et al. "Extraction, Identification and Quantitation of Succinylcholine in Embalmed Tissue." *Journal of Analytical Toxicology* 6.3 (1982): pp. 115-19. May 1, 1982.

King, Wayne. "Investigators Near End of Inquiry Into Deaths of Infants at Hospital." *New York Times.* April 11, 1984.

King, Wayne. "Questions on Infant Deaths Beset San Antonio Hospital." *New York Times.* July 2, 1983.

Moore, Kelly and Dan Reed. *Deadly Medicine.* St. Martin's Press, 1988.

"Nurse Gets 60 Years For Injuring Texas Child." *New York Times.* October 25, 1984.

Riley, Joyce. *The Power Hour.* Genesis Communications Network. Aired February 22, 2013.

Venema, Paul. "Survivor of 'Killer Nurse' Opposes Her Planned Release." *KSAT 12 News.* May 22, 2013

Chapter 11: Ray & Faye Copeland

"Deadly Harvest." *Killer Trials: Judgment Day.* Investigation Discovery, Season 1 Episode 4. Aired Feb 17, 2012.

Miller, Tom. *The Copeland Killings.* Pinnacle True Crime, 1993. Print.

"Rural Intrigue Is Unearthed With 5 Bodies." *New York Times,* November 25, 1989.

Tackett, Michael. "Trial Starts In Farmhand Slayings." *Chicago Tribune.* March 8, 1991.

Thomas, Sindy. Personal interview. 26 February 2018.

Chapter 12: Evan (Continued)

Allington, Adam. "Opioid Overdoses Overwhelm the Nation's Morgues." *Marketplace.* American Public Media. May 11, 2017, 2:00 PM. Radio and Web.

Heron, Melonie, PhD *National Vital Statistics Reports.* Centers for Disease Control and Prevention. Vol. 65, No. 5, "Deaths: Leading Causes for 2014." June 30, 2016.

Leonard, Kimberly. "These Are the Drugs Killing the Most People in the US" *US News and World Report.* December 20, 2016. Web.

Thomas, Sindy. Personal interview. 26 February 2018.

Woodward, Joseph. Personal interview. 26 February 2018.

Chapter 13: Kevin Foster

Dunbar, Patricia Schwebes. "Lords of Chaos convicted killer gets clemency denied." *Barefoot Preachr* [sic].. March 6, 2011. Web.

Greenhill, Jim. *Someone Has to Die Tonight.* Kensington, 2006. Print.

"Lords of Chaos." *Arrest & Trial.* Aired in Syndication, Nov 21, 2000.

"Lords of Chaos." *In the Line of Duty.* Volume 2, Episode 10. Production date unknown.

Motz, Timothy. *"Lords of Chaos Leader Gets Death."* *Naples Daily News.* June 18, 1998.

Schone, Mark. "Redneck Nation." *Spin Magazine.* Februrary 1997.

Ulene, Valerie, MD "A teen's friends are a powerful influence." *Los Angeles Times.* April 11, 2011.

"When a Killer Calls." *Dateline NBC.* NBC. December 2, 2006. Television.

Chapter 14: Theresa Knorr

1960 US Census.

"A Mother's Love." *Wicked Attraction*. Investigation Discovery. Season 2, Episode 4. 2009. Television.

Blackburn, Matthew. "Behind Closed Doors: The Secret Life of the Knorr Family." *The Line-Up*. 12 August 2015. Accessed June 20, 2016. Web.

Clarkson, Wensley. *Whatever Mother Says…A True Story of a Mother, Madness and Murder*. St. Martin's Griffin, 1995. Print.

Knorr Walker, Terry. Facebook page. Accessed 23 June 2016. Web.

McDougal, Dennis. *Mother's Day*. Fawcett, 1995.

Paddock, Richard C. "Police Finally Believe Tale of Depravity and Murder." *The Spokesman Review* reprinting *Los Angeles Times*. November 15, 1993.

Paddock, Richard C. " 'Unbelievable' Tale Reveals Grisly Crimes." *Los Angeles Times*. November 14, 1993.

"Sacred Bond." *Deadly Women*. Discovery Channel. Season 4, Episode 7. 2010. Television.

"Theresa Marie 'Terry' Knorr Walker." *FindAGrave.com*. Accessed 23 June 2016. Web.

Chapter 15: Carlette Parker

"Carlette Parker." *Killer Medics on Death Row*. Crime + Investigation Television Australia. Season 1, Episode 1. Television.

Hawco, Stephanie. "Woman Charged with Kidnapping Makes First Court Appearance Today." *WRAL*. May 15, 1998. Radio.

Springmoor Life Care Retirement Community Disclosure Statement (October 1, 2016; received by gov't Oct 17 2016; accessed May 9, 2017).

"State v. Parker." *FindLaw*. Supreme Court of North Carolina. No. 556A99, November 9, 2001.

"State v. Parker." *North Carolina Reports: Cases Argued and Determined in the Supreme Court of North Carolina, Vol. 354*. Supreme Court of North Carolina. 354 N.C. 268, 2001.

Wright, Kelly. "Care Giver Trust May Have Been Broken in Covington Death." *WRAL*. May 17, 1998.

Chapter 16: Dennis Rader

"31 Years of the BTK Killer." *Dateline NBC*. NBC, aired August 24, 2005. Television.

"BTK: Out of the Shadows." *CBS News*. CBS, aired September 29, 2005. Television.

"BTK Strangler." *Crimes that Shook the World*. IWC Media, aired Oct 6, 2006. Television.

"BTK Took Body to Church, Says Investigator." *CNN.com Law Center*. August 18, 2005. Web.

Douglas, John and Johnny Dodd. *Inside the Mind of BTK: The True Story Behind the Thirty-Year Hunt for the Notorious Wichita Serial Killer*. Jossey-Bass, 2008. 376 pp. Print.

Green, Jaime. "Former Police Officer Went From Coaching BTK to Catching Him." *Wichita Eagle*. September 20, 2014. Web.

I Survived BTK: BTK and the Otero Family Murders. Dir.: Marc Levitz. UNSUB Films, 2010. Film.

Kansas v. Dennis L. Rader. "State's Summary of the Evidence." Eighteenth Judicial District Court, Sedgwick County, Kansas. Case No. 05 CR 498. August 18, 2005.

Kansas v. Dennis L. Rader. "Transcript of Sentencing Hearing, Vols. I–VI." Eighteenth Judicial District Court, Sedgwick County, Kansas. Case No. 05 CR 498. August 17–18, 2005.

Miller, Kenneth. "Surviving the BTK Killer." *Reader's Digest*. August 2008.

Ramsland, Katherine. *Confession of a Serial Killer: The Untold Story of Dennis Rader, the BTK Killer*. ForeEdge, 2016. Print.

Wenzl, Roy. "Book Shows BTK as 'Selfish, Egotistical Bastard.' " *Wichita Eagle*. August 18, 2016.

Wenzl, Roy. "When Your Father Is the BTK Serial Killer, Forgiveness Is Not Tidy." *Wichita Eagle*. February 21, 2015.

Wenzl, Potter, et al. *Bind, Torture, Kill: The Inside Story of BTK, the Serial Killer Next Door*. Harper, 2008.

Chapter 17: Dennis Hastert

Arnold, Chris. "Disgraced Former House Speaker Dennis Hastert Reports To Prison." *National Public Radio*. June 22, 2016. Web.

Davey, Monica. "US Accuses Ex-House Speaker J. Dennis Hastert of Paying to Hide 'Misconduct.' " *New York Times*. May 28, 2015. Web.

Davey, Monica; Bosman, Julie; Smith, Mitch. "Dennis Hastert Sentenced to 15 Months, and Apologizes for Sex Abuse." *New York Times*. April 27, 2016. Web.

Hastert, Dennis. *Speaker: Lessons from Forty Years in Coaching and Politics*. Regnery Press, 2004. Print.

James Doe v. John Dennis Hastert. L35 Circuit Court for the 23rd Judicial Circuit, Kendall County, Illinois. 2015.

Lipton, Eric; Davey, Monica. "Wrestling Propelled Hastert's Career, and Provided Opportunity for Abuse." *New York Times*. April 22, 2016. Web.

Marans, Daniel. "Patriot Act That Dennis Hastert Passed Led To His Indictment." *Huffington Post*. May 28, 2015. Web.

Mencimer, Stephanie. "Dennis Hastert May Have Chosen the Absolute Worst Way to Buy Someone's Silence." *Mother Jones*. June 8, 2015. Web.

Ornstein, Norm. "Worse Than FoleyGate." *American Enterprise Institute*. October 6, 2016. Web.

Ornstein, Norm. "This Isn't Dennis Hastert's First Scandal." *The Atlantic*. June 3, 2015. Web.

Phillips, Amber. "Former House Speaker Dennis Hastert Just Reported to Jail. Here's How He Got There." *Washington Post*. June 22, 2016. Web.

Terkel, Amanda and Stein, Sam. "Dennis Hastert Hid His Skeletons As He Helped Push GOP's Anti-Gay Agenda." *Huffington Post.* June 6 2015. Web.

United States of America v. John Dennis Hastert. US District Court, Northern District of Illinois, Eastern Division. 2015.

US House of Representatives. *Committee on Standards of Official Conduct Investigation of Allegations Related to Improper Conduct Involving Members and Current or Former House Pages.* December 8, 2006.

Zapotosky, Mark. " 'He apparently had no fears': The steep, unexpected downfall of Dennis Hastert." *Washington Post.* April 24, 2016. Web.

Conclusion

"Face the Facts." *The Next Door.* Nashville, TN. May 17, 2017. Web.

Wadhwani, Anita. "How Opioids Took Hold of Tennessee." *The Tennessean.* USA Today Network. March 26, 2017. May 17, 2017. Web.

Woodward, Joseph. Personal interview. 26 February 2018.

ABOUT THE AUTHOR

—

Eric Brach is a lecturer in English at West Los Angeles College, where he works with members of the LAPD in leading a career and technical education program for students interested in the field of law enforcement.

He has written for everyone from *Bleacher Report* to *The Onion*, and he penned the screenplay for the Nintendo Wii game *Mushroom Men*.

His previous non-fiction books include *Billy the Hill and the Jump Hook*, about Utah basketball legend Billy McGill, and *Conquering the Electron*, a detailed study of the intersection between technological innovation and business acumen.